Addiction

Other Books of Related Interest:

At Issue Series

Mexico's Drug War

Current Controversies Series

Prescription Drugs

Introducing Issues with Opposing Viewpoints Series

Drug Legalization

Issues That Concern You Series

Medical Marijuana

"Congress shall make no law . . . abridging the freedom of speech, or of the press."

First Amendment to the US Constitution

The basic foundation of our democracy is the First Amendment guarantee of freedom of expression. The Opposing Viewpoints series is dedicated to the concept of this basic freedom and the idea that it is more important to practice it than to enshrine it.

| Addiction

Christine Watkins, Book Editor

GREENHAVEN PRESS
A part of Gale, Cengage Learning

Farmington Hills, Mich • San Francisco • New York • Waterville, Maine
Meriden, Conn • Mason, Ohio • Chicago

Elizabeth Des Chenes, *Director, Content Strategy*
Cynthia Sanner, *Publisher*
Douglas Dentino, *Manager, New Product*

© 2014 Greenhaven Press, a part of Gale, Cengage Learning

WCN: 01-100-101

LIBRARY OF CONGRESS CATALOGING-IN-PUBLICATION DATA

Addiction / Christine Watkins, book editor.
        p. cm. -- (Opposing viewpoints)
    Includes bibliographical references and index.
    ISBN 978-0-7377-6941-8 (hardcover) -- ISBN 978-0-7377-6942-5 (pbk.)
    1. Substance abuse. 2. Interpersonal relations. I. Watkins, Christine, 1951- editor of compilation.
    HV4998.A319 2014
    362.29--dc23
                                                    2013036319

Printed in the United States of America
1 2 3 4 5 6 7 18 17 16 15 14

Contents

Chapter 3: How Do Addictions Affect Relationships?

Chapter 4: How Can Addictions Be Treated?

Why Consider Opposing Viewpoints?

> *"The only way in which a human being can make some approach to knowing the whole of a subject is by hearing what can be said about it by persons of every variety of opinion and studying all modes in which it can be looked at by every character of mind. No wise man ever acquired his wisdom in any mode but this."*
>
> *John Stuart Mill*

In our media-intensive culture it is not difficult to find differing opinions. Thousands of newspapers and magazines and dozens of radio and television talk shows resound with differing points of view. The difficulty lies in deciding which opinion to agree with and which "experts" seem the most credible. The more inundated we become with differing opinions and claims, the more essential it is to hone critical reading and thinking skills to evaluate these ideas. Opposing Viewpoints books address this problem directly by presenting stimulating debates that can be used to enhance and teach these skills. The varied opinions contained in each book examine many different aspects of a single issue. While examining these conveniently edited opposing views, readers can develop critical thinking skills such as the ability to compare and contrast authors' credibility, facts, argumentation styles, use of persuasive techniques, and other stylistic tools. In short, the Opposing Viewpoints Series is an ideal way to attain the higher-level thinking and reading skills so essential in a culture of diverse and contradictory opinions.

In addition to providing a tool for critical thinking, Opposing Viewpoints books challenge readers to question their own strongly held opinions and assumptions. Most people form their opinions on the basis of upbringing, peer pressure, and personal, cultural, or professional bias. By reading carefully balanced opposing views, readers must directly confront new ideas as well as the opinions of those with whom they disagree. This is not to argue simplistically that everyone who reads opposing views will—or should—change his or her opinion. Instead, the series enhances readers' understanding of their own views by encouraging confrontation with opposing ideas. Careful examination of others' views can lead to the readers' understanding of the logical inconsistencies in their own opinions, perspective on why they hold an opinion, and the consideration of the possibility that their opinion requires further evaluation.

Evaluating Other Opinions

To ensure that this type of examination occurs, Opposing Viewpoints books present all types of opinions. Prominent spokespeople on different sides of each issue as well as well-known professionals from many disciplines challenge the reader. An additional goal of the series is to provide a forum for other, less known, or even unpopular viewpoints. The opinion of an ordinary person who has had to make the decision to cut off life support from a terminally ill relative, for example, may be just as valuable and provide just as much insight as a medical ethicist's professional opinion. The editors have two additional purposes in including these less known views. One, the editors encourage readers to respect others' opinions—even when not enhanced by professional credibility. It is only by reading or listening to and objectively evaluating others' ideas that one can determine whether they are worthy of consideration. Two, the inclusion of such viewpoints encourages the important critical thinking skill of objectively evaluating an author's credentials and bias. This evaluation will illuminate an author's reasons for taking a particular stance on an issue and will aid in readers' evaluation of the author's ideas.

It is our hope that these books will give readers a deeper understanding of the issues debated and an appreciation of the complexity of even seemingly simple issues when good and honest people disagree. This awareness is particularly important in a democratic society such as ours in which people enter into public debate to determine the common good. Those with whom one disagrees should not be regarded as enemies but rather as people whose views deserve careful examination and may shed light on one's own.

Thomas Jefferson once said that "difference of opinion leads to inquiry, and inquiry to truth." Jefferson, a broadly educated man, argued that "if a nation expects to be ignorant and free . . . it expects what never was and never will be." As individuals and as a nation, it is imperative that we consider the opinions of others and examine them with skill and discernment. The Opposing Viewpoints series is intended to help readers achieve this goal.

David L. Bender and Bruno Leone,
Founders

Introduction

"While experts do not all agree about behavioral addictions being considered real addictions, they do all agree that the kinds of behavior that are prone to excess can bring with them negative consequences, including problems with relationships, finances, work, or other areas of life." Elizabeth Hartney, "Are Behavioral Addictions Real?" About.com, March 26, 2010.

Addiction is a hot topic among Americans these days. According to Alva Noë, a philosophy professor at the University of California, Berkeley, in a 2011 article on the National Public Radio website, "Addiction has been moralized, medicalized, politicized, and criminalized." Experts and researchers have long haggled over how and why addiction develops, whom it affects, and even what it encompasses. For example, the American Society of Addiction Medicine (ASAM) considers addiction to be a primary illness not caused by mental health issues. Husband and wife psychoanalysts Morteza Khaleghi and Karen Khaleghi, however, believe that addiction is indeed a result of mental health issues. In their book, *The Anatomy of Addiction: Overcoming the Triggers That Stand in the Way of Recovery*, they write, "There is always—*always*—a contextual reason for addiction. Perhaps some traumatic event or some physiological or psychological disease preceded the addiction and, years and even decades later, still causes hurt and distress the sufferer seeks to salve." Some experts believe environmental factors and overwhelming stress can lead to addiction, while others believe it is caused by genetic factors. Further adding to the mix of dissention is the issue of whether certain behaviors, such as gambling or shopping, should be considered addictions. While *Merriam-Webster's Collegiate Dictionary* defines addiction as a "compulsive need for and use of a habit-forming substance (as heroin, nicotine, or alcohol) characterized by tolerance and by well-defined physiological symptoms upon withdrawal," many experts have expanded the definition to include habit-forming behaviors and activities as well as substances. In fact, when the American Psychiatric Association (APA) revised its *Diagnostic and Statistical Manual of Mental Disorders* (DSM) in 2013, it included a new section for behavioral addictions. This is a significant modification that will greatly affect public health policy and addiction treatment because insurance companies must comply with DSM diagnostic categories in deciding which treatments to cover.

As scientists and researchers increase their knowledge of how certain behaviors affect neurotransmitters in the brain—most notably the neurological reward system—they are coming to accept the theory that compulsive behaviors once viewed as moral weaknesses or impulse-control problems should be considered medical disorders. According to Noë, "One strategy is to look not to the substances and activities themselves, but to the effects that they produce in addicts. And here neuroscience has delivered important insights." In his book, *High Stakes: The Rising Cost of America's Gambling Addiction*, journalist Sam Skolnik explains, "The rush gamblers crave is the high that's felt when a bet is made, and sometimes when the gambler is just anticipating making the bet. Blood surges to the face. The mouth dries up. Concentration narrows as time seems to slow. The high is fleeting but is repeated as soon as the next bet is made. . . . The experience has been compared to snorting a line of cocaine." Underscoring this line of thinking, the ASAM is adamant that any addiction, whether behavioral or substance related, is a chronic disease of the brain: "Addiction is not about drugs; it's about brains. Addiction is about what happens in a person's brain when they are exposed to rewarding substances or rewarding behaviors."

Not everyone agrees, however, that compulsive behaviors should be diagnosed as addictions. The rationale behind the behavior-addiction theory is that compulsive behaviors affect neurotransmission within the reward circuits of the brain in the same clinical pattern as do addictive drugs. As psychologist John M. Grohol explains on his website, Psych Central, "everything we do affects these areas of the brain; especially anything we personally find enjoyable—like most of us do when socializing with other people (whether in person or online). When we are having an enjoyable conversation with another person, it leads to a biological and behavioral response. We can even 'crave' talking to that person again, since we often make a date to see that person again. None of these things are necessarily unique to addiction." Psychiatrist Allen Frances also sees a fundamental problem with the idea of behavior addictions. In a 2012 article on the Huffington Post website, he writes, "Pleasure seeking is a ubiquitous part of human nature. . . . Potentially millions of new 'patients' would be created by fiat, medicalizing all manner of impulsive, pleasure-seeking behaviors and giving people a 'sick role' excuse for impulsive irresponsibility." Perhaps most importantly, unintended consequences may result from allowing behaviors to be diagnosed as addictions. In an article in the Fall 2010 newsletter of the California Society of Addiction Medicine, Reef Karim, a professor at the Semel Institute for Neuroscience and Human Behavior at the University of California, Los Angeles, writes, "Where do we draw the line between an excessive bad behavior and a true addiction? . . . Further, adding more diagnostic disorders may increase the general public's suspicion of the validity of psychiatric disorders in general."

The debate regarding behavioral addictions is only one of many surrounding the complicated subject of addiction. Other controversies include the brain disease model of addiction, effective prevention programs for adolescents, and drug rehabilitation facilities. This book examines society's attitudes about addiction, and in the following chapters experts and others discuss the effects of addiction on society and debate what reforms should be undertaken.

CHAPTER 1

What Are Some Causes and Sources of Addiction?

Chapter Preface

Overwhelming emptiness, agitation, abnormal sleep patterns, paranoia, "itching like a crackhead." These are all sensations that people experience when forced to forgo the use of the Internet or other technological media devices, according to several recent surveys conducted by various universities and technology companies. One such global study by the International Center for Media & the Public Agenda (ICMPA) asked university students in 2010 to abstain from using technology-based devices for twenty-four hours; one of the participating students reported afterward, "I am an addict. I don't need alcohol, cocaine, or any other derailing form of social depravity. . . . Media is my drug; without it I was lost." Another survey by the technology firm TeleNav revealed that more than half of Americans would rather give up chocolate, alcohol, and caffeine for a week than give up—even temporarily—the use of their phones.

What has been called "Internet addiction" or IAD, is difficult to define. Compulsive use of the Internet or other technological devices to the point that it interferes with regular life activities (maintaining personal relationships, going to work, or practicing personal hygiene) is a characteristic of the definition. But the addict also builds up a tolerance for usage and may experience psychological withdrawal symptoms, such as depression, anger, and anxiety, as well as physical symptoms, such as rapid heartbeat and shortness of breath. In fact, scientists discovered altered reward systems in the brains of technology addicts similar to that of drug addicts. In his book, *iDisorder: Understanding Our Obsession with Technology and Overcoming Its Hold on Us*, Larry Rosen writes, "A recent study of brain tissue in adolescents afflicted with Internet addiction leaves no doubt that there are differences between addicts and non-addicts in terms of brain systems. The researchers found that there were significant differences in the gray matter and white matter—measures related to the structure and functions of neurons—between the addicted adolescents and their 'healthy' counterparts."

This dependence on technology can have a serious effect on relationships—"real" relationships as opposed to digital ones. Actual face-to-face human contact and verbal communication via the telephone is decreasing. Adults sitting around a table in a restaurant can be seen actively engaged with their cell phones instead of talking to each other. Computers, iPads, and stimulating apps are becoming substitute babysitters. Attention spans are getting shorter and shorter. In a 2012 article for the *Observer* newspaper, Tracy McVeigh writes, "In China, Taiwan, and Korea, Internet addiction is accepted as a genuine psychiatric problem with dedicated treatment centres for teenagers who are considered to have serious problems with their web use. Next year, America's *Diagnostic and Statistical Manual of Mental Disorders*, the authority on mental illness, could include 'Internet use disorder' in its official listings."

What, if anything, should be done about the public's captivation with technology and media devices? After all, the Internet has brought a lot of good into people's lives and plays a vital role in today's world. Technology experts and psychiatrists believe that finding a balance is key. Richard Fernandez, Google's development director, agrees and says that teaching people to occasionally disconnect is vital: "Consumers need to have an internal compass where they're able to balance the capabilities that technology offers them for work with the qualities of the lives they live offline." Perhaps Singyin Lee gives the best advice in an article on the website HongKiat.com: "When your digital devices are taking up too much of your life, you know it's time to switch it off and enjoy live unplugged."

> "I only wish that when I was younger I could've understood what alcoholism really is—a genetic mutation, a mental illness, and a lifelong battle."

Addiction Stems from a Genetic Disorder

Nic Sheff

Nic Sheff is a columnist for the Fix, *an addiction and recovery website, and the author of two memoirs about his struggles with alcoholism and drug addiction. According to Sheff, his addictions arose from a genetic mutation that causes him to be prone to addictive tendencies. He maintains that alcohol and drugs altered his brain chemistry to the extent that he became a lifelong addict. The following viewpoint is an excerpt from Sheff's second book,* We All Fall Down: Living with Addiction.

As you read, consider the following questions:

1. According to Nic Sheff, will an addict's natural instinct for survival help deter the craving for drugs?

2. Does Sheff believe that the amount of drugs used has any effect on a person's ability to sober up?

3. According to Sheff, could awareness of a genetic vulnerability to addiction help in the prevention of addiction?

It's October 2011 . . . a little over three years since me 'n' Justin were living together in that apartment in East Hollywood.

It's been three years, and by some f—— miracle, I've been sober all the while, and, crazily enough, Justin is about to graduate from law schooL

Well, I don't know, maybe it's not just a miracle.

I mean, I've done a lot of work, too, learning how to love and accept myself—building up a life that I actually want to fight for. Trying and trying and trying again.

Holding on.

Not giving up.

Fighting.

Fighting for the life I have today.

'Cause I do . . . I fight for it.

Every day I take the different medications I've been prescribed.

Every day I go running with Tallulah and Rhett, my little baby bloodhound, up in the canyons around Los Angeles.

Every day I write and try to build a life for myself.

Every day I pay my bills and clean my apartment and eat dinner and try 'n' sleep.

Every day I live sober.

I travel around talking to high school kids about addiction and recovery. I go to therapy with Dr. Cooper. I write a column about recovery for an online magazine, thefix.com. I don't drink. 1 don't do drugs.

It is every day.

And it never ends.

Addiction is a lifelong process for me. And as much as I do love my life today, I still wouldn't wish this thing on anyone. Being an addict sucks.

When I go to high schools and talk to kids, I always tell them, you know, it may look like I went through everything and came out the other side okay and even successful, but that's not how it is at all. Every day I suffer from the decisions I made and from this addiction thing that I allowed to get so out of control.

From the ages of eleven to twenty-six, I've been wasting my life trying to figure out a way to not have to be sober. I just did not want to accept the fact that I have this alcoholism thing and it is a death sentence—no, worse than a death sentence. It's worse than a death sentence 'cause it manipulated me and made me crazy and delusional and it altered my brain chemistry so I am left permanently damaged.

For so long I tried to blame my addiction on my family or my childhood or my depression and bipolar disorder, but that was all just bullshit.

It's taken me a long time to understand what's really wrong with me.

You see, there's a scientist—some lady in San Francisco—who's been able to breed an entire strain of addict flies. That is, flies that are drug addicts/alcoholics. The way I understand it is that this scientist created an alcohol-and-cocaine vapor that the flies could inhale if they chose to walk down a certain corridor in their cage. And she, the scientist, found that, while all the flies will, from time to time, go down the corridor to get drunk or high—a smaller percentage of the population will go down the corridor over and over again—abandoning all food and water—participating in a cycle that seems eerily human. They get drunk or stoned, wobble around for a while, have trouble flying, and pass out for twenty or thirty minutes, and then they wake up and do it all over again.

And so by examining and dissecting those particular flies more prone to addictive tendencies, that scientist has actually been able to isolate some of the genes linked with alcoholism and then breed those particular flies with those genes together in order to create an entire, like, brood of alcoholic/addict flies. In fact, these flies are such hard-core addicts that even when the corridor leading to their drug supply is replaced with a highly electrified metal panel, the flies will still walk down it to get their drug of choice. Sure they'll be getting shocked to all hell, but it still won't stop them. Whereas the nonaddict flies will put one little fly foot on that electrified surface and then back off immediately, never to go back.

The addict flies, just like addict humans, will go to absolutely any lengths to get their next fix—even when that is in direct opposition to what is every living creature's natural instinct for survival and self-preservation. In other words, once an addict is an addict—that is, an active addict—whether you're a human being or a gross-ass fly, getting high is the only thing that matters. We will do anything it takes to get more. It becomes what we live for. And that is not a moral or rational decision. It is encoded in our DNA. And, yes, it can remain dormant for your whole life. Or it can awaken like it did for me—you know, back when I was twelve years old and I'd started smoking pot every day.

So that means the drugs actually were the problem—well, the drugs and my g———d——— genetic code....

It's ridiculous, really, to think about how long I've fought to deny that simple fact. And, honestly, I'm not even sure why that is exactly. Maybe it just seemed embarrassing to admit that it was the drugs themselves that totally f——— up my life. Like, it seemed cooler or whatever to be able to blame my addiction on my messed-up childhood, or my creepy stepdad, or my mom leaving, or something like that. And, while I'm sure all that stuff did play a role in terms of why I started using drugs in the first place, my actual addiction had nothing to do with any of that. 'Cause obviously a ton of people have a hard time growing up, and obviously they don't all turn out to be drug addicts—even the ones who end up doing drugs.

The only thing that made me any different was that I had this messed-up genetic whatever, just like my new little fly friends. And then the drugs did the rest. The drugs changed me. They changed my brain chemistry, and they even changed the way I thought about myself and my past.

Back when I was eighteen and I first tried crystal meth, I remember having this feeling like, wow, this is the first and only time I've ever been happy. And I believed that. Hell, I believed that for most of my life. I believed that before crystal meth I was never happy—and that without crystal, I would never be happy again.

But that was a lie.

That was a lie that the drug told me.

That lie was the drug manipulating me and changing my brain chemistry. And, yeah, like the flies, I learned to walk across an electrified panel just to get another fix.

It's pathetic, I know.

I take a drink or a drug and instantly I start to turn.

I become a man becoming a fly.

Me and the flies, operating from the same place of blind, insatiable hunger.

There's a scene in that [director David] Cronenberg [1986] movie—you know, *The Fly*—where [actor] Jeff Goldblum (midway through fly transformation) tells [actress] Geena Davis, "I'm an insect who dreamt he was a man and loved it. But now the dream is over . . . and the insect is awake."

And, yeah, the more drugs I use—and the longer I'm out there—the more g——d—— fly-like I become—and the harder it is to get back to my humanness.

And I know that not everybody is able to make it back.

I only wish that when I was younger I could've understood what alcoholism really is—a genetic mutation, a mental illness, and a lifelong battle. Maybe then I would've been able to recognize the signs of my own budding alcoholism before my whole life was taken over.

Targeting Treatments for People at Risk

As more genes are linked to the development of alcohol dependence, these insights will be used to improve tools for gauging an individual's risk for developing alcoholism and identifying those with alcohol problems who may respond better to specific treatments. Doctors commonly consider a person's genetic profile and other family and environmental risk factors when combining medications and behavioral prescriptions for complex conditions such as hypertension, cancer and bipolar affective disorder. Clinicians are in the earliest stages of using genetic variants to shape treatment decisions for alcoholism, and in the future we expect to have molecular guidelines to help develop such individualized strategies.

The recent genetic findings related to alcoholism may also suggest ways to improve the prevention and treatment of smoking and other forms of substance dependence that are frequently seen in people with alcohol problems and tend to cluster in the same families. Mood and anxiety disorders fall into this category as well, and the association between [gene] variations, alcoholism and depression illustrates how these problems may stem in part from a common source. Improved understanding of alcohol dependence should therefore help dissect factors involved in the development of related conditions.

John I. Nurnberger Jr. and Laura Bierut,
"Seeking the Connections: Alcoholism and Our Genes,"
Scientific American, vol. 296, no. 4, April 2007.

Maybe I wouldn't have had to waste all those years living as a g——d—— fly.

It was just such a waste.

The only reconciliation I have with any of this is that I have the opportunity now to share what I've learned and to hopefully help other addicts.

Not that I'm ungrateful for my life now.

Because I am. I am grateful.

All I'm saying is that it's a waste.

And there's nothing glamorous or sexy about that.

It's not cool or badass.

What's cool is being able to take care of your family.

What's badass is being able to give your family a home and health insurance and being able to pay your taxes.

What's glamorous is being a good father, a good husband, a good f—— dog owner.

That's what I care about today.

That's what matters.

I will devote everything to that.

And I will succeed.

Because I cannot fall down again.

I will not fall down again.

I mean, I don't have to fall.

None of us have to fall.

We don't all fall down.

We don't.

So I'm over this drug shit.

It's done.

And this is my last recovery memoir ever.

That is, I'll have no more drug stories to tell after this.

But I am gonna keep on writing. In fact, I'm working on a novel right now, and I've even been doing some TV writing.

And while it's not gonna be about drugs ... there'll definitely be plenty of blood and sex and gore in everything I do to go around. ....

So hopefully y'all will wanna keep checkin' my stuff out.

Like Marc Bolan says,

"Deep in my heart,

there's a house
that can hold
just about all of you."
All right, cool, thanks again. . . .
Talk to you soon. . . .

| "The early environment, consisting of both the prenatal and postnatal periods, has a profound effect on gene expression and adult patterns of behavior."

Addiction Stems from Early Environment

Gabor Maté

In the following viewpoint, Gabor Maté explains that despite the current consensus that a predisposition for addiction is determined by a person's genetic makeup, it is actually a person's early environment that influences how genes function. Maté further explains that maternal stress—both during and after pregnancy—affects a broad range of a child's emotional and behavioral patterns, including addiction. Gabor Maté is a noted physician, researcher, public speaker, columnist, and author. The following viewpoint is an excerpt from his book, In the Realm of Hungry Ghosts: Close Encounters with Addiction.

Excerpted from *In the Realm of Hungry Ghosts: Close Encounters with Addiction,* by Gabor Maté, M.D. Copyright © 2008 Gabor Maté. Reprinted by permission of Knopf Canada. From *In the Realm of Hungry Ghosts: Close Encounters with Addiction,* by Gabor Maté, American edition published by North Atlantic Books through cooperation with Random House Canada, copyright © 2010 by Gabor Maté. Reprinted by permission of publisher.

As you read, consider the following questions:

1. What is the focus of epigenetics, according to Gabor Maté?

2. According to Maté, what is the name of the hormone that can damage an infant's brain if the mother is highly stressed?

3. Why are adoption studies unreliable for determining genetic causation of addiction, according to Maté?

Whatever problem we are hoping to resolve or prevent—be it war, terrorism, economic inequality, a marriage in trouble, climate change, or addiction—the way we see its origins will largely determine our course of action. I present the case that the early environment plays a major role in a person's vulnerability to addiction not to exclude genetics but to counter what I see as an imbalance. Genes certainly appear to influence, among other features, such traits as temperament and sensitivity. These, in turn, have a huge impact on how we experience our environment. In the real world there is no nature versus nurture argument, only an infinitely complex and moment-by-moment interaction between genetic and environmental effects. For this reason, as two psychiatrists at the University of Pittsburgh School of Medicine have pointed out, "the liability trait for alcoholism is not static." Owing to developmental and environmental factors, "the risk of alcoholism fluctuates over time." Even if, against all available evidence, it were demonstrated conclusively that 70 percent of addiction is programmed by our DNA, I would still be more interested in the remaining 30 percent. After all, we cannot change our genetic makeup, and at this point, ideas of gene therapies to change human behaviors are fantasies at best. It makes sense to focus on what we *can* immediately affect: how children are raised, what social support parenting receives, how we handle adolescent drug users, and how we treat addicted adults.

Exaggerated Statistics for Genetic Causation

The current consensus—among those who accept a high degree of hereditary causation for alcoholism—is that predisposition to the disorder is about 50 percent genetically determined. Equally extravagant estimates are applied to other addictions. Heavy marijuana use is said to be 60 to 80 percent heritable, while the inherited liability to long-term heavy nicotine use has been calculated to be an astonishing 70 percent. Cocaine abuse and dependence are also reported to be "substantially influenced by genetic factors." Some researchers have even suggested that alcoholism and divorce may share the same genetic propensity.

Such high figures are beyond possibility. The logic behind them rests on mistaken assumptions that owe less to science than to an exaggerated belief in the power of genes to determine our lives. In genetic theories of mental disorders, "unscientific beliefs play a major role," write the authors of a research review. . . .

The Theory of Epigenetics

There is a new and rapidly growing science that focuses on how life experiences influence the function of genes. It's called *epigenetics*. As a result of life events, chemicals attach themselves to DNA and direct gene activities. The licking of a rat pup by the mother in the early hours of life turns on a gene in the brain that helps protect the animal from being overwhelmed by stress even as an adult. In rats deprived of such grooming, the same gene remains dormant. Epigenetic effects are most powerful during early development and have now been shown to be transmittable from one generation to the next, without any change in the genes themselves. Environmentally induced epigenetic influences powerfully modulate genetic ones.

How a gene acts is called *gene expression*. It is now clear that "the early environment, consisting of both the prenatal

Blaming Biology Is Not the Solution

From gambling addiction to information addiction, petting your dog addiction to surfing the internet addiction, all addictions are a choice as a way to medicate yourself from not feeling any uncomfortable feelings. Just like with alcohol, there has never been found a chocolate addiction gene, a text message addiction gene or even a shopping addiction gene. . . .

Most of us have never learned how to feel our feelings so we have found ways to mask those feelings. That is what all addictions do—mask feelings. Addictions are a relationship with something that we have chosen to cover up our emotions. An addiction could be a substance (like alcohol), an emotion, a behavior, a thought, a person or an object that is used to hide one's feelings. Nowhere in the equation is there any errant gene, biological allergy or failure of the body.

Jon Burras, "Is Alcoholism a Disease?"
JonBurras.com, March 2011.

and postnatal periods, has a profound effect on gene expression and adult patterns of behavior," to quote a recent [2005] article from the *Journal of Neuroscience*. . . .

The Factor of Maternal Stress

Numerous studies in both animals and humans have found that maternal stress or anxiety during pregnancy can lead to a broad range of problems in the offspring, from infantile colic to later learning difficulties and the establishment of behavioral and emotional patterns that increase a person's predilection for addiction. Stress on the mother would result in higher levels of cortisol reaching the baby; and . . . chronically elevated cortisol is harmful to important brain structures especially during periods of rapid brain development. A recent British study, for example, found that children whose mothers were stressed during pregnancy are vulnerable to mental and behavioral problems like attention deficit/hyperactivity disorder (ADHD) or to being anxious or fearful. (ADHD and anxiety are powerful risk factors for addiction.) "Professor Yvette Glover of Imperial College London found stress caused by rows with or violence by a partner was particularly damaging," noted a BBC [British Broadcasting Corporation] report. "Experts blame high levels of the stress hormone cortisol crossing the placenta. Professor Glover found high cortisol in the amniotic fluid bathing the baby in the womb tallied with the damage." The study's results are consistent with previous evidence that stress on the mother during pregnancy affects the brain of the infant, with long-term and perhaps permanent effects. . . .

It has been demonstrated that both animals and humans who experienced the stress of their mothers during pregnancy are more likely to have disturbed stress-control mechanisms long after birth, which creates a risk factor for addiction. Maternal stress during pregnancy can, for example, increase the offspring's sensitivity to alcohol. . . . A relative scarcity of dopamine receptors also elevates the addiction risk. "We've done work, and a lot of other people have done work, showing that essentially the number and density of dopamine receptors in these receptive areas is determined in utero," [says] psychiatric researcher Dr. Bruce Perry. . . .

For these reasons, adoption studies cannot decide questions of generic inheritance. Any woman who has to give up her baby for adoption is, by definition, a stressed woman. She is stressed not just because she knows she'll be separated from her baby but primarily because if she wasn't stressed in the first place, she would never have had to consider giving up her child: the pregnancy was unwanted or the mother was poor, single, or in a bad relationship; or she was an immature teenager who conceived involuntarily or was a drug user or was raped or confronted by some other adversity. Any of these situations would be enough to impose tremendous stress on any person, and so for many months the developing fetus would be exposed to high cortisol levels through the placenta. A proclivity for addiction is one possible consequence. . . .

Genetics As an Excuse

Why, then, are narrow genetic assumptions so widely accepted and, in particular, so enthusiastically embraced by the media? The neglect of developmental science is one factor. Our preference for a simple and quickly understood explanation is another, as is our tendency to look for one-to-one causations for almost everything. Life in its wondrous complexity does not conform to such easy reductions.

There is a psychological fact that, I believe, provides a powerful incentive for people to cling to genetic theories. We human beings don't like feeling responsible: as individuals for our own actions; as parents for our children's hurts; or as a society for our many failings. Genetics—that neutral, impassive, impersonal handmaiden of Nature—would absolve us of responsibility and of its ominous shadow, guilt. If genetics ruled our fate, we would not need to blame ourselves or anyone else. Genetic explanations get us off the hook. The possibility does not occur to us that we can accept or assign responsibility without taking on the useless baggage of guilt or blame.

Evading Proactivity

More daunting for those who hope for scientific and social progress, the genetic argument is easily used to justify all kinds of inequalities and injustices that are otherwise hard to defend. It serves a deeply conservative function: if a phenomenon like addiction is determined mostly by biological heredity, we are spared from having to look at how our social environment supports, or does not support, the parents of young children and at how social attitudes, prejudices, and policies burden, stress, and exclude certain segments of the population and thereby increase their propensity for addiction. The writer Louis Menand said it well in a *New Yorker* [magazine] article:

> "It's all in the genes": an explanation for the way things are that does not threaten the way things are. Why should someone feel unhappy or engage in antisocial behavior when that person is living in the freest and most prosperous nation on earth? It can't be the system! There must be a flaw in the wiring somewhere.

Succumbing to the common human urge to absolve ourselves of responsibility, our culture has too avidly embraced genetic fundamentalism. That leaves us far less empowered to deal either actively or proactively with the tragedy of addiction. We ignore the good news that nothing is irrevocably dictated by our genes and that, therefore, there is much we can do.

| *"Brain changes occur as a matter of everyday life; the brain can be changed by the choice to think or behave differently."*

Addiction Is a Choice, Not a Disease

Steven Slate

In the following viewpoint, Steven Slate argues that the brain disease concept of addiction is false because the evidence provided by disease proponents—brain scans showing abnormal changes in neuronal pathways and circuitry—does not hold up to scrutiny. Slate maintains that changes in the brain are perfectly normal and can actually occur through one's own volition. Steven Slate, a former substance abuser, is the author of the website The Clean Slate Addiction Site. *He works in research and development with the Baldwin Research Institute in New York City.*

As you read, consider the following questions:

1. According to Steven Slate, various areas of the brain grow and expand or become less active depending on the amount of use. What is the term that refers to this ability of the brain to change its structure?

2. The author contends that physical activity can rewire the brains circuits, but does he believe that thoughts alone can also affect the brain?

3. If the brain can be changed into an addicted state, is it possible to reverse the changes, according to the author?

In a true disease, some part of the body is in a state of abnormal physiological functioning, and this causes the undesirable symptoms. In the case of cancer, it would be mutated cells which we point to as evidence of a physiological abnormality; in diabetes we can point to low insulin production or cells which fail to use insulin properly as the physiological abnormality which create the harmful symptoms. If a person has either of these diseases, they cannot directly choose to stop their symptoms or directly choose to stop the abnormal physiological functioning that creates the symptoms. They can only choose to stop the physiological abnormality indirectly, by the application of medical treatment, and in the case of diabetes, dietetic measures may also indirectly halt the symptoms as well (but such measures are not a cure so much as a lifestyle adjustment necessitated by permanent physiological malfunction).

Brain Scans as Proof That Addiction Is a Disease

In addiction, there is no such physiological malfunction. The best physical evidence put forward by the disease proponents falls totally flat on the measure of representing a physiological malfunction. This evidence is the much touted brain scan. The organization responsible for putting forth these brain scans, the National Institute on Drug Abuse and Addiction (NIDA), defines addiction in this way:

Addiction is defined as a chronic relapsing brain disease that is characterized by compulsive drug seeking and use, despite harmful consequences. It is considered a brain disease because drugs change the brain—they change its structure and how it works. These brain changes can be long lasting, and can lead to the harmful behaviors seen in people who abuse drugs.

They are stating outright that the reason addiction is considered a disease is because of the brain changes evidenced by the brain scans they show us, and that these changes cause the behavior known as addiction, which they characterize as "compulsive drug seeking and use". There are two ways in which this case for the disease model falls apart:

- The changes in the brain they show us are not abnormal at all.

- There is no evidence that the behavior of addicts is compulsive (compulsive means involuntary).

This all applies equally to "alcoholism" as well.

Brain Changes in Addicts Do Not Prove the Brain Disease Theory

On the first count—the changes in the brain that we see in the brain scans of substance abusers are not an abnormal functioning of the brain. They are quite normal, as research into neuroplasticity has shown us. Whenever we practice doing or thinking anything enough, the brain changes—different regions and neuronal pathways are grown or strengthened, and new connections are made. Various areas of the brain become more or less active depending upon how much you use them, and this becomes the norm in your brain, but changes again as you adjust how much you use those brain regions depending on what you choose to think and do. This is a process that continues throughout life, and there is nothing abnormal about it. But don't take my word for it. Listen to Sharon Begley, science writer for the *Wall Street Journal*, who has spent years investigating and writing both newspaper columns and books on this principle known as neuroplasticity.

> The term [neuroplasticity] refers to the brain's recently discovered ability to change its structure and function, in particular by expanding or strengthening circuits that are used and by shrinking or weakening those that are rarely engaged. In its short history, the science of neuroplasticity has mostly documented brain changes that reflect physical experience and input from the outside world.

So, when the NIDA's [director] Nora Volkow and others show us changes in the brain of a substance user as compared to a non-substance user, this difference is not as novel as they make it out to be. They are showing us routine neuroplastic changes which every healthily functioning person's brain goes through naturally. The phenomenon of brain changes isn't isolated to addicts or anyone else with a so-called brain disease—non-addicted and non-depressed and non-[insert brain disease of the week here] people experience brain changes too. One poignant example was found in the brains of London taxi drivers, as Begley and neuroscientist Jeffrey Schwartz pointed out in [their book] *The Mind and The Brain*.

Physiological Brain Changes Are Normal

A specific area of the brain's hippocampus is associated with creating directional memories and a mental map of the environment. A team of researchers scanned the brains of London taxi drivers and compared their brains to non-taxi drivers. There was a very noticeable difference, not only between the drivers and non-drivers, but also between the more experienced and less experienced drivers.

> There it was: the more years a man had been a taxi driver, the smaller the front of his hippocampus and the larger the posterior. "Length of time spent as a taxi driver correlated positively with volume in ... the right posterior hippocam-

pus," found the scientists. Acquiring navigational skills causes a "redistribution of gray matter in the hippocampus" as a driver's mental map of London grows larger and more detailed with experience.

So, the longer you drive a cab in London (that is, the longer you exert the mental and physical effort to quickly find your way around one of the world's toughest-to-navigate cities), the more your brain physically changes. And the longer you use drugs, the more your brain changes. And indeed, the longer and more intensely you apply yourself to any skill, thought, or activity—the more it will change your brain, and the more visible will be the differences between your brain and that of someone who hasn't been focused on that particular skill. So, if we follow the logic of the NIDA, then London's taxi drivers have a disease, which we'll call taxi-ism. But the new diseases wouldn't stop there.

Learning to play the piano well will change your brain— and if you were to compare brain scans of a piano player to a non-piano player, you would find significant differences. Does this mean that piano playing is a disease called Pianoism? Learning a new language changes your brain—are bilingual people diseased? Athletes' brains will change as a result of intensive practice—is playing tennis a disease? Are soccer players unable to walk into a sporting goods store without kicking every ball in sight? We could go on and on with examples, but the point is this—when you practice something, you get better at doing it, because your brain changes physiologically, and this is a normal process. If someone dedicated a large portion of their life to seeking and using drugs, and their brain didn't change—then that would be a true abnormality. Something would be seriously wrong with their brain.

Changing the Brain Can Be a Matter of Choice

It's not just physical activity that changes our brains, thoughts alone can have a huge effect. What's more, whether the brain changes or not, there is much research which shows that the brain is slave to the mind. . . .

Purely mental activity can change the brain in physiologically significant ways. And to back up this fact, Dr. Gene Heyman [in his book *Addiction: A Disorder of Choice*] brings up the case of Dr. Jeffrey Schwartz, who has taught OCD [obsessive-compulsive disorder] patients techniques to think their way out of obsessive thoughts. After exercising these thought practices, research showed that the brains of OCD patients looked no different than the brains of those who never had OCD. If you change your thoughts, you change your brain physically—and this is voluntary. This is outside the realm of disease, this shows a brain which changes as a matter of normality, and can change again, depending on what we practice. There is nothing abnormal about a changing brain, and the types of changes we're discussing aren't necessarily permanent, as they are characterized to be in the brain disease model of addiction.

These brain changes don't need to be brought on by exposure to chemicals. Thoughts alone, are enough to rewire the very circuits of the human brain responsible for reward and other positive emotions that substance use and other supposedly "addictive" behaviors ("process addictions" such as sex, gambling, and shopping, etc.) are connected with.

Brain Changes Can Be Reversed

Those who claim that addiction is a brain disease readily admit that the brain changes in evidence are arrived at through repeated choices to use substances and focus on using substances. In this way, they are saying the disease is a product of routine neuroplastic processes. Then they go on to claim that such brain changes either can't be remedied, or can only be remedied by outside means (medical treatment). . . . If neuroplasticity is involved and is a valid explanation for how to become addicted, then we can't act is if the same process doesn't

The "Compulsion Excuse" for Addiction in Criminal Cases

Few people are compelled to become addicted. Peer pressure to experiment may be common in adolescence and early adulthood, but it seldom takes a form that would justify a compulsion excuse. Initial use is almost always intentional and in most cases rational because virtually no one is immediately hooked or harmed (and most people who use frequently are not addicts or generally endangered). The user tries the substance to please friends, for the thrill of experimenting or being on the edge, for the pleasure or arousal the substance produces, and for a host of other reasons that do not suggest excusing irrationality. Moreover, almost no one is literally forced to become an addict by the involuntary administration of substances. In conclusion, most people who become addicts may fairly be held responsible to a substantial degree for becoming addicted.

Stephen J. Morse, "Addiction and Criminal Responsibility,"
Addiction and Responsibility, *edited by Jeffrey Poland
and George Graham. Cambridge, MA: MIT Press, 2011.*

exist when it's time to focus on getting un-addicted. That is, if the brain can be changed into the addicted state by thoughts and choices, then it can be further changed or changed back by thoughts and choices. Conditions that can be directly remedied by freely chosen thoughts and behaviors don't fit into the general understanding of disease. Ultimately, if addiction is a disease, then it's a disease so fundamentally different than any other that it should probably have a completely different name that doesn't imply all the things contained in the term "disease"—such as the idea that the "will" of the afflicted is irrelevant to whether the condition continues.

Substance Use Is Not Compulsive

On the second count, is there any evidence that substance use is involuntary? When the case for the disease is presented, the idea that drug use is involuntary is taken for granted as true. No evidence is ever actually presented to support this premise, so there isn't much to be knocked down here, except to make the point I made above—is a piano player fundamentally incapable of resisting playing the piano? They may love to play the piano, and want to do it often, they may even be obsessive about it, but it would be hard to say that at the sight of a piano they are involuntarily driven by their brain to push aside whatever else they need to do in order to play that piano.

There is evidence that shows people don't lose control though. A series of well-designed experiments throughout the '60s and '70s established this fact. These were called "priming dose" experiments, and the method the researchers used was to trick alcoholics into drinking alcohol without knowing it. The researchers then measured the alcoholics' level of craving for alcohol, and they even made more of the supposedly non-alcoholic beverages available to drink. The alcoholics didn't drink or crave uncontrollably when they were unaware that they had ingested alcohol. This result clearly defies the expectations of the disease model. Additionally, in some variations of the priming dose experiments, the researchers gave some test subjects non-alcoholic drinks, but told them that it contained alcohol. In these cases, they proceeded to drink more than the alcoholics who drank alcohol without knowing it.

When reviewing the results of 9 separate priming dose experiments in their book *Controlled Drinking*, researchers Nick Heather and Ian Robertson concluded that "drinking behaviour conventionally described as loss of control is mediated by cognitive processes and not by a physico-chemical reaction to ethanol." Or in simpler terms, heavy substance use is a choice based on thoughts—it's not an involuntary behavior triggered by the power of a chemical over a diseased brain.

There is another approach to the second claim though. We can look at the people who have subjectively claimed that their substance use is involuntary and see if the offer of incentives results in changed behavior. Heyman covered this in his latest book, *Addiction: A Disorder of Choice*. He recounts studies in which cocaine abusers were given traditional addiction counseling, and also offered vouchers which they could trade in for modest rewards, such as movie tickets or sports equipment—if they proved through urine tests that they were abstaining from drug use. In the early stages of the study, 70% of those in the voucher program remained abstinent, while only 20% stayed abstinent in the control group that didn't receive the incentive of the vouchers. This demonstrates that substance use is not in fact compulsive or involuntary, but that it is a matter of choice, because these "addicts" when presented with a clear and immediately rewarding alternative to substance use and incentive not to use, chose it. Furthermore, follow up studies showed that this led to long-term changes. A full year after the program, the voucher group had double the success rate of those who received only counseling (80% to 40%, respectively). This ties back in to our first point that what you practice, you become good at. The cocaine abusers in the voucher group practiced replacing substance use with other activities, such as using the sports equipment or movie passes they gained as a direct consequence of abstaining from drug use—thus they made it a habit to find other ways of amusing themselves. This probably led to brain changes, and the new habits became the norm.

Long story short, there is no evidence presented to prove that substance use is compulsive. The only thing ever offered is subjective reports from drug users themselves that they can stop, and proclamations from treatment professionals that the behavior is compulsive due to brain changes. But if the promise of a ticket to the movies is enough to double the success rate of conventional addiction counseling, then it's hard to say that substance users can't control themselves. The reality is that they can control themselves, but they just happen to see substance use as the best option for happiness available to them at the times when they're using substances. When they can see other options for happiness as more attractive (i.e. as promising a greater reward than substance use), attainable to them, and as taking an amount of effort they're willing to expend—then they will absolutely choose those options instead of substance use, and will not struggle to stay sober, prevent relapse, practice self-control or self-regulation, or any other colloquialism for making a different choice. They will simply choose differently.

Two Most Relevant Reasons Addiction Is Not a Disease

So to sum up, there are at least two significant reasons why the current brain disease theory of addiction is false.

A disease involves physiological malfunction; the "proof" of brain changes shows no malfunction of the brain. These changes are indeed a normal part of how the brain works—not only in substance use, but in anything that we practice doing or thinking intensively. Brain changes occur as a matter of everyday life; the brain can be changed by the choice to think or behave differently. And the type of changes we're talking about are not permanent.

Drug use in addicts is not compulsive. If it were truly compulsive, then offering a drug user tickets to the movies would not make a difference in whether they use or not—because this is an offer of a choice. Research shows that the offer of this choice leads to cessation of substance abuse. Furthermore, to clarify the point, if you offered a cancer patient movie tickets as a reward for ceasing to have a tumor—it would make no difference, it would not change his probability of recovery.

Addiction is NOT a disease. . . .

When we accept the unproven view that addiction and alcoholism are brain diseases, then it will lead us down a long, painful, costly, and pointless road of cycling in and out of ineffective treatment programs and 12-step meetings. You will waste a lot of time without finding a permanent solution. When we examine the evidence, throw out the false disease concepts, and think rationally about the problem, we can see that addiction is really just a matter of choice. Knowing this, we can bypass the rehabs and find the true solution within ourselves. You can choose to end your addiction. You can choose to improve your life. You can choose to stop the endless cycle of "recovery" and start living. You don't need to be a victim of the self-fulfilling prophecy that is the brain disease model of addiction.

> *"Four lines of evidence all substantiate that marijuana is addictive: basic neuroscience, animal studies, clinical reports of human experience with marijuana, and epidemiology."*

Marijuana Use Is Addictive

California Society of Addiction Medicine

The California Society of Addiction Medicine (CSAM), the California chapter of the American Society of Addiction Medicine (ASAM), is a professional society representing physicians dedicated to increasing access and improving the quality of addiction treatment, education, and research. In the following viewpoint, CSAM maintains that strong scientific evidence collected through animal studies and clinical research proves that marijuana has all the characteristics of an addictive drug. CSAM further contends that the rate of marijuana dependence can triple for those who use marijuana before the age of eighteen.

As you read, consider the following questions:

1. What is the final common pathway in the brain that is activated by all drugs of addiction, according to the CSAM?

2. According to the CSAM, every drug known to cause addiction promotes an increase in what organic compound in the brain?

3. Common symptoms of marijuana withdrawal include anger or aggression and decreased appetite. According to the CSAM, what are two less-common symptoms?

Four lines of evidence all substantiate that marijuana is addictive: basic neuroscience, animal studies, clinical reports of human experience with marijuana, and epidemiology. Data from these four areas of scientific research corroborate each other and interweave fluidly to dispel the myth that marijuana is not addictive.

In order to place the following information in its proper perspective, medicine's current understanding of how marijuana interacts with the brain needs to be outlined. Scientific research has discovered an extensive system of nerves within the brain that communicate with each other using the same basic chemistry found in marijuana. The THC (tetrahydrocannabinol) and similar molecules in marijuana are able to affect the brain by mimicking our natural neurotransmitters and flooding receptor sites with stimulation. All the cannabinoid-based areas of the brain are subsequently activated beyond normal physiological levels by using marijuana.

While we are only beginning to unravel the pervasive role the endocannabinoid (i.e., the brain's naturally occurring THC-like molecules) system plays in overall brain function, Raphael Mechoulam, one of the most important pioneers in cannabinoid research, has declared that "The cannabinoid receptors are found in higher concentrations than any other receptor in the brain. . . and the endocannabinoid system acts essentially in just about every physiological system that people have looked into, so it appears to be a very central system."

Effect of Marijuana on the Reward Center

The brain's Reward Center (Nucleus Accumbens) is the final common pathway activated by all drugs of addiction. Normally, the Reward Center experiences a rise in dopamine in response to behaviors that bear repeating (eating, exercising, sexual activity, novelty) to promote survival. By a wide variety of mechanisms, every drug known to cause addiction promotes an increase in dopamine in the Reward Center, often by a full order of magnitude (10X) higher than is normally found physiologically. While this increase in dopamine is not the whole story of addiction, it is the hallmark of addictive drugs (e.g., nicotine, caffeine, alcohol, benzodiazepines, opiates, stimulants, etc.). . .

The Reward Center contains cannabinoid receptors and the natural endocannabinoid chemistry to stimulate them. Ingesting marijuana leads to a rise in dopamine and alters the rate of nerve cell firing in the Reward Center of a magnitude similar to that caused by others addictive drugs. If a cannabinoid blocker is administered first, the THC contained in marijuana no longer causes a rise in dopamine, demonstrating the direct effect of marijuana on the Reward Center. Chronic administration of THC eventually alters both the sensitivity and the structure of connections (synapses) within the Reward Center.

Animal Studies Pertaining to Marijuana Addiction

One of the gold standards for demonstrating the behaviors characteristic of addiction is to develop an animal (i.e., nonhuman) model; in other words, can it be demonstrated that animals will self-administer marijuana? This has been accomplished with squirrel monkeys that had never been exposed to psychoactive drugs previously. Both the THC found in marijuana and the brain's natural endocannabinoid (anandamide) effectively reinforce a monkey's pushing a level to self-administer an intravenous dose. Similar results with mice and rats have been obtained.

Animal models have also been developed for studying withdrawal from cannabinoid addiction. After being administered THC (or a variety of similar cannabinoid drugs) via injection on a daily or twice daily basis for a week, animals have been given a cannabinoid blocker (SR141716A), an antagonist that is capable of stopping all cannabinoid activity in the brain. The antagonist has little or no impact when given by itself. But, when the brain has been primed by a week of THC administration, SR141716A suddenly precipitates a recognizable pattern of withdrawal symptoms: diarrhea, vomiting, increased aggressiveness, and increases in restless behavior and trembling, head shaking and sleep disruption (with EEG disturbances). Similar signs of withdrawal have been demonstrated across a variety of species. Although more exaggerated by having withdrawal precipitated, on the face of things these withdrawal symptoms appear to resemble spontaneous reports by humans in early abstinence from chronic marijuana use.

Although the focus of this article is on the addictive potential of marijuana, attention should also be paid to multiple other ways that the brain is altered by chronic use. For example, the number of cannabinoid receptor sites, and therefore the sensitivity of the brain to its own endocannabinoid chemistry, is reduced in areas outside the Reward Center by as much as 70%.

Clinical Reports of Withdrawal in Humans

Human beings almost never ingest a cannabinoid blocker and so do not experience precipitous withdrawal from marijuana. The fact that THC is a fatty acid and is only gradually released from the body's fat stores after an individual becomes abstinent also contributes to the lack of precipitous withdrawal. The question remains, however, whether any symptoms of withdrawal (and therefore of physical addiction) occur in humans, and what significance these symptoms would have if they are present.

Especially after improvements in the THC content of marijuana became widely available, controlled studies of heavy smokers in abstinence began to find significant increases in anxiety, irritability, physical tension, and decreases in mood and appetite during marijuana withdrawal. Chronic marijuana users display more aggressive behavior on days 3 and 7 of marijuana abstinence, continuing for as long as 28 days. Adolescents voluntarily seeking treatment for cannabis dependence have reported restlessness, appetite change, and cravings, irritability, depression, twitches and shakes, and perspiring.

Proposed Marijuana Withdrawal Syndrome

Alan Budney [a professor of psychiatry at the Geisel School of Medicine at Dartmouth College] has organized the symptoms of marijuana withdrawal into the following proposed formal diagnostic framework:

Common symptoms (reported by > 70% of abstinent individuals)

- Anger or aggression
- Decreased appetite or weight loss
- Irritability
- Nervousness/anxiety
- Restlessness
- Sleep difficulties, including strange dreams

Less common symptoms/equivocal symptoms

- Chills
- Depressed mood

- Stomach pain

- Shakiness

- Sweating

A strong relationship exists between relapses from marijuana abstinence in response to intolerance of one or more of these withdrawal symptoms.

Criteria for Marijuana Addiction

Measurements of the frequency of substance abuse (high risk use) and substance dependence are usually based on the diagnostic criteria established in DSM-IV—the *Diagnostic and Statistical Manual* used to define psychiatric illnesses. These criteria can be summarized as follows:

- Tolerance/Withdrawal

- Loss of Control

- Preoccupation with the drug

- Continued Use in the Face of Adverse Consequences

- Cognitive Distortions/Denial

In 2007, 14.4 million Americans aged 12 or older used marijuana at least once in the month prior to being surveyed. Of those individuals who initiate marijuana use at 18 years or older, approximately 9% eventually satisfy DSM criteria for dependence. Rates of cannabis dependence are estimated at 20% to 30% among those who have used at least five times, and even higher estimates (35%–40%) are reported among those who report near daily use. For those who use marijuana before age 18, the rate of dependence can triple, depending on how early use begins. Marijuana dependence also develops more quickly in adolescents, with up to 17% becoming addicted within the first two years of use.

| "There is little scientific evidence to substantiate the notion that marijuana use permanently or significantly damages the brain."

Harmful Effects of Marijuana Use Are Exaggerated

Paul Armentano

In the following viewpoint, Paul Armentano maintains that moderate marijuana use poses little threat to public health and, in fact, enhances relaxation and concentration. He further contends that marijuana is not only nontoxic, but may also reduce the risk of various types of cancer. Paul Armentano is the deputy director of NORML, the National Organization for the Reform of Marijuana Laws. His writing and research regarding marijuana appears in academic textbooks and anthologies, and he is the coauthor of the book, Marijuana Is Safer, So Why Are We Driving People to Drink?

As you read, consider the following questions:

1. Approximately what time period did the cultivation and use of marijuana begin, according to Paul Armentano?

2. According to Armentano, do all the active chemicals in marijuana induce euphoria?

3. Does marijuana use have a long-term effect on learning and memory, according to Armentano?

Humans have cultivated and consumed marijuana since virtually the beginning of recorded history. Cannabis-based textiles dating to 7,000 B.C.E. have been recovered in northern China, and the plant's use as a medicinal and euphoric agent date back nearly as far. In 2008, archeologists in Central Asia discovered over two pounds of cannabis in the 2,700-year-old grave of an ancient shaman. After scientists conducted extensive testing on the material's potency, they concluded, "[T]he most probable conclusion . . . is that [ancient] culture[s] cultivated cannabis for pharmaceutical, psychoactive, and divinatory purposes."

Today [2011] over 17,000 studies pertaining to the marijuana plant, its unique active constituents (cannabinoids), and the human body's own marijuana-like chemicals (endocannabiods) exist in the scientific literature. We now know far more about cannabis than most foods we eat or pharmaceutical drugs we ingest.

Just what exactly do we know? The consistent conclusion drawn by the available scientific literature is that cannabis, when consumed in moderation by adults, poses little threat to public health. . . .

Marijuana's Impact on the Body

The physical, therapeutic, and psychoactive effects one experiences after ingesting marijuana are derived primarily from a family of unique chemicals in the plant known as cannabinoids. Of the dozens of cannabinoids in marijuana, only one—THC—is significantly psychoactive. Most active chemicals in the plant possess therapeutic properties but do not induce euphoria. Some compounds, most specifically the cannabinoid cannabidiol (CBD) counteract the psychoactive properties of THC, acting as marijuana's "anti-marijuana" mechanism.

The reason a person experiences psychological, therapeutic, or physical effects after ingesting marijuana is largely because cannabinoids interact with individual receptors, so-called CB1 and CB2 receptors, located throughout the body. The CB1 receptors reside predominantly in the brain and regulate the drug's psychoactive effects. The CB2 receptors are located throughout the human body, and play a role in regulating many of the cannabinoids' therapeutic effects.

Because the majority of the body's CB1 receptors are located in the frontal lobe region of the brain's cerebral cortex (which regulates emotional behavior) and the cerebellum (a region in the back of the brain that primarily controls motor coordination), but not the brain stem (which controls life-preserving functions like breathing), ingesting marijuana is believed to be pharmacologically incapable of causing a fatal overdose, regardless of dosage or THC potency. According to a 1995 report prepared for the World Health Organization, "There are no recorded cases of overdose fatalities attributed to cannabis, and the estimated lethal dose for humans extrapolated from animal studies is so high that it cannot be achieved by recreational users."

The specific psychological, therapeutic, and physical effects experienced after consuming marijuana vary from person to person, and many of these effects are dependent on the percentage of THC or other cannabinoids present in the marijuana consumed. Moreover, cannabis naive users tend to feel different effects compared with more experienced users. For example, if an inexperienced user consumes too much cannabis at one time, they may experience a mix of unpleasant physical and psychological feelings, such as a tachycardia (rapid heart beat), dry mouth, and a growing sense of paranoia. (These adverse effects are commonly referred to as a "panic attack.") Fortunately these feelings, while mildly unpleasant, are only temporary and pose little-to-no actual long-term risk to the users' health.

As cannabis consumers become more experienced, they become more tolerant to some of the drug's physical effects. Users also learn to better self-regulate (or "titrate") their dosage to avoid any dysphoric symptoms such as paranoia. As a result, most experienced marijuana consumers describe the cannabis high as a pleasant experience that helps them to relax, socialize or unwind.

Recently, investigators at the University of Alberta, Canada, conducted a series of lengthy interviews with male and female cannabis consumers to better determine why adults use marijuana. They reported that the majority of individuals who use cannabis recreationally do so to "enhance relaxation." Researchers concluded: "[M]ost adult marijuana users regulate use to their recreational time and do not use compulsively. Rather, their use is purposively intended to enhance their leisure activities and manage the challenges and demands of living in contemporary modern society. Generally, participants reported using marijuana because it enhanced relaxation and concentration, making a broad range of leisure activities more enjoyable and pleasurable."

Marijuana Use Versus Alcohol Use

Throughout history, alcohol and marijuana have been the two most popular social relaxants consumed by western civilizations. Yet the risks posed by marijuana and alcohol—both to the individual consumer and to society as a whole—are far from equal. For example, a 2009 report published in the British Columbia Mental Health and Addictions journal *Visions* estimated, "In terms of [health-related] costs per user: tobacco-related health costs are over $800 per user, alcohol-related health costs are much lower at $165 per user, and cannabis-related health costs are the lowest at $20 per user."

Why the dramatic discrepancy? Quite literally, alcohol is an intoxicant; cannabis is not.

The word *intoxicant* is derived from the Latin noun, *toxicum*, meaning: "a poison." It's an appropriate description for booze. Alcohol is toxic to healthy cells and organs, a side effect that results directly in some 35,000 deaths per year from illnesses like cirrhosis, ulcers, and heart disease. Furthermore ethanol, the psychoactive ingredient in beer, wine, and hard liquor, is carcinogenic. Following ethanol's initial metabolization by the body it is converted to acetaldehyde. This is why even moderate drinking is positively associated with increased incidences of various types of cancer, including cancers of the breast, stomach, liver, esophagus, and pancreas. Heavy alcohol consumption can depress the central nervous system—inducing unconsciousness, coma, and death—and is strongly associated with increased risks of injury. According to the U.S. Centers for Disease Control, alcohol plays a role in about 41,000 fatal accidents per year. Alcohol consumption also plays a primary role in the commission of acts of violence. In fact, according to the federal Bureau of Justice Statistics, alcohol consumption plays a role in the commission of approximately one million violent crimes annually.

Marijuana's Healing Abilities

By contrast, cannabinoids are remarkably non-toxic. Unlike alcohol, marijuana is incapable of causing fatal overdose and its use is inversely associated with aggression and injury. Unlike alcohol, the use of cannabis is not linked to increased risk of mortality or various types of cancer—including lung cancer—and may even reduce such risk. For instance, a 2009 study in the journal *Cancer Prevention Research* reports that moderate use of marijuana is associated with "a significantly reduced risk of head and neck squamous cell carcinoma."

A separate 2006 population case-control study, funded by the U.S. National Institutes of Health and conducted by the

The Gateway Theory

The clear impression is that marijuana, alcohol, and tobacco more often than not *cause* drug users to graduate up to LSD, cocaine, and heroin, perhaps by altering their brain chemistry. This "gateway theory" has been around for decades....

The idea that smoking pot leads to snorting cocaine and shooting heroin is also unsupported by the government's own statistics. Each year, the Substance Abuse and Mental Health Services Administration conducts something of a census of drug users to get a picture of who is using what illegal substance and how frequently. If the gateway theory were to hold up, one would expect to see the number of monthly pot users either equal to or less than the number of cocaine and heroin users. But the opposite is true: In 2009, 15.2 million Americans were estimated to be "past-month" pot smokers, while only an estimated 1.8 million are past-month cocaine users and a mere 213,000 past-month users of heroin. Even if every heroin and cocaine user identified in the study began using those hard drugs because they smoked pot, that means that 85 percent of pot smokers haven't.

Greg Campbell, *Pot, Inc.:*
Inside Medical Marijuana, America's Most Outlaw Industry.
Toronto, Canada: Sterling, 2012.

University of California at Los Angeles, also reported that lifetime use of cannabis was not positively associated with cancers of the lung or aerodigestive tract, and further noted that certain moderate users of the drug experienced a reduced cancer risk compared to non-using controls. Finally, a 1997 retrospective cohort study of 65,000 examinees by Kaiser Permanente concluded, "Compared with nonusers/experimenters (lifetime use of less than seven times), ever and current use of marijuana were not associated with increased risk of cancer, [including] . . . tobacco-related cancers or with cancer of the following sites: colorectal, lung, melanoma, prostate, breast, [or] cervix."

In 2011, the website of the National Cancer Institute, a branch of the federal government, acknowledged: "Cannabinoids may cause antitumor effects by various mechanisms, including induction of cell death, inhibition of cell growth, and inhibition of tumor angiogenesis and metastasis. Cannabinoids appear to kill tumor cells but do not affect their non-transformed counterparts and may even protect them from cell death."

Marijuana's Impact on the Brain

There is little scientific evidence to substantiate the notion that marijuana use permanently or significantly damages the brain. In adults, cannabis consumption is not associated with residual deficits in cognitive skills, as measured by magnetic resonance imaging, neurocognitive performance testing, or fMRI [functional magnetic resonance imaging] imaging.

Most recently, Harvard Medical School researchers performed magnetic resonance imaging on the brains of long-term cannabis users (reporting a mean of 20,100 lifetime episodes of smoking) and controls (subjects with no history of cannabis use). Imaging displayed "no significant differences" between heavy marijuana smokers compared to non-smokers.

Additional clinical trials have reported similar results. An October 2004 study published in the journal *Psychological Medicine* examined the potential adverse effects of marijuana on cognition in monozygotic [identical] male twins. It reported "an absence of marked long-term residual effects of marijuana use on cognitive abilities." Likewise, a 2002 clinical trial published in the *Canadian Medical Association Journal* determined, "Marijuana does not have a long-term negative impact on global intelligence."

Though a handful of studies have reported that long-term users sometimes perform differently than non-users on certain cognitive tests immediately after ceasing their cannabis use, these same studies report that both former users and non-users test similarly within a matter of days. Notably, a 2001 study published in the journal *Archives of General Psychiatry* found that long-term cannabis smokers who abstained from the drug for one week "showed virtually no significant differences from control subjects (those who had smoked marijuana less than 50 times in their lives) on a battery of 10 neuropsychological tests." Investigators further added, "Former heavy users, who had consumed little or no cannabis in the three months before testing, [also] showed no significant differences from control subjects on any of these tests on any of the testing days."

Most recently, a just-published study [researched] nearly 2,000 young Australian adults "for eight years and found that marijuana has little long-term effect on learning and memory—and any cognitive damage that does occur as a result of cannabis use is reversible.". . .

Marijuana's Legal Status

Marijuana is not a harmless substance—no potentially mind-alerting substance is. But this fact is precisely why its commercial distribution ought to be controlled and regulated by the state in a manner similar to the licensed distribution of alcohol and cigarettes—two legal substances that cause far greater harm to the individual user and to society as a whole than cannabis ever could.

The above findings demonstrate that any risk presented by marijuana smoking falls within the ambit of choice we should permit the individual in a free society.

> "Online gaming is an emotionally drain-
> ing and time-consuming activity. To
> create more time for the computer,
> gaming addicts neglect sleep, diet, exer-
> cise, hobbies, and socializing."

Online Game Playing Can Be Addictive

Kimberly Young

*In the following viewpoint, Kimberly Young maintains that on-
line gaming is a fast growing form of addiction, especially among
children and teenagers. Young explains that classic signs of addiction include a preoccupation with gaming, a loss of interest in
other activities, and withdrawal from family and friends. Kimberly Young is a psychologist and the founder of the Center for
Internet Addiction. She is also the author of* Caught in the Net:
How to Recognize the Signs of Internet Addiction—and a
Winning Strategy for Recovery.

As you read, consider the following questions:

1. According to Kimberly Young, what problem can result
   when young people spend hours pretending to be a
   character in an online game?

Kimberly Young, "Understanding Online Gaming Addiction and Treatment Issues for
Adolescents." *The American Journal of Family Therapy*, vol. 37, Taylor & Francis, Ltd.,
2009, pp. 355–372. Reprinted by permission of the publisher (Taylor & Francis Ltd,
http://www.tandf.co.uk/journals).

2. What are two physical health problems that gaming addicts can develop, according to Young?

3. What damage can occur as multiuser gamers form intimate bonds with one another, according to Young?

Over the last decade [since the late 1990s], the concept of Internet addiction has grown in terms of its acceptance as a legitimate clinical disorder often requiring treatment. Hospitals and clinics have emerged with outpatient treatment services for Internet addiction, addiction rehabilitation centers have admitted new cases of Internet addicts, and college campuses have started support groups to help students who are addicted.

Excessive Gaming

The Internet is a new technology that has impacted the world and provided many benefits to its users. At the same time the Internet has had negative ramifications. Some people are becoming preoccupied with the Internet, are unable to control their use, and are jeopardizing employment and relationships. The concept of "Internet addiction" has been proposed as an explanation for uncontrollable, damaging use of this technology.

Studies on Internet addiction originated in the United States. More recently, studies have documented Internet addiction in a growing number of countries such as Italy, Pakistan, and Czech Republic. Reports also indicate that Internet addiction, especially to online games has become a serious public health concern in China, Korea, and Taiwan. About 10 percent of China's more than 30 million Internet gamers were said to be addicted. To battle what has been called an epidemic, Chinese authorities regularly shut down Internet cafes and instituted laws to limit the number of hours adolescents can play online games.

Excessive gaming has been identified as a specific subtype of Internet addiction. It is difficult to estimate how widespread the problem is, but according to the American Medical Association, up to 90 percent of American youngsters play video games and as many as 15 percent of them—more than 5 million children—may be addicted. Problems stemming from online games have become so serious that the first Detox Center for Video Game Addiction opened in the Netherlands. "Video games may look innocent, but they can be as addictive as gambling or drugs and just as hard to kick," explained Keith Bakker, director of Amsterdam-based Smith&Jones Addiction Consultants and founder of the center.

Virtual Worlds

To understand online gaming addiction, it is important to understand how the addiction stems from the creation of virtual worlds. New studies have shown that immersion into online games allows users to become addicted.

In the 1980s, games such as Centipede, Space Invaders, Pac Man, and Donkey Kong were popularized. These were single-player games against the machine and getting good at the game only meant a high score and improvement of the gamers' eye-hand coordination. By the 1990s, gaming evolved from single-player games to gaming *experiences*. Gamers could become immersed in a virtual world that they helped to create. Games such as Doom and Quake were introduced that allowed players to create new rooms, customize their characters, and specify the kinds of weapons used. As the gaming revolution evolved, players could create rich, malleable environments from designer-generated fantasies to complex Hollywood movie themes. By the late 1990s, the gaming industry exploded. Manufacturers such as Sony and Microsoft have developed more sophisticated and interactive features into their games and the technology has become much more portable and mobile making online games accessible anytime and anywhere.

Online games evolved into more than games but rather they are living, self-contained three-dimensional societies. Each game has its own scenery from forests, prairies, beaches, mountains, and towns. Players can immerse themselves and collectively evolve in these virtual worlds. Each game has its own currency to buy goods and services. Gold, coins, jewels, bears, or pelts may be used to buy weapons, armor, or magical potions, depending upon the economics and currency of the game. To play, players first create a "character," or a virtual version of themselves. The player must decide a character's race, its species, history, heritage, and philosophy. The genres and themes vary, as a player could be a greedy business type in one game, a strong warrior in another game, or an elf with magical powers in another.

As online gaming evolved so have the forms that characters can take, so that players can select more detailed representations for their characters. For instance, for human characters, players can select skin color, hair color, height, weight, and gender. They also can decide on a character's profession, ranging from a banker, lawyer, dancer, engineer, thief, bounty hunter, elf, or gnome, depending upon the game. Each player must choose a name for the character. Some take great care and pride in determining just the right name. In fact, in some strange way, a character's name seeps into the player over time. They spend hours living as this "other person" and begin to identify with a character that feels more real and less fictional the longer they play.

[Research scientist Nick] Yee . . . suggested that hardcore players tend to be younger players who may suffer from emotional problems or low self worth and esteem. He suggested that individuals who have other emotional problems may be more at risk to develop an addiction to interactive gaming. In the game, these interactive environments allow individuals to experiment with parts of their personality, they can be more vocal, try out leadership roles, and new identities. The problem becomes when these younger players rely upon these new online personas and the distinction between what is real and what is a fantasy becomes blurred.

Playing for Hours

In one of the most dramatic stories of online gaming addiction, in August 2005, a 28-year-old South Korean man died— not by committing suicide, but after playing the game Starcraft at an Internet cafe for 50 hours straight. By all reports, the man had not slept properly and had eaten very little in that time. While no autopsy was performed, he was believed to have died from heart failure stemming from exhaustion.

An addiction to online games can cause a tremendous amount of consequences to the gamer. Gaming addicts willingly forgo sleep, food, and real human contact just to experience more time in the virtual world. Gaming addicts sometimes play for ten, fifteen, or twenty hours straight in a single gaming session, every day. Because of the complexity of the game, players are constantly stimulated in an ever-changing virtual environment. "Just a few more minutes" can turn into hours as the gaming addict searches for the next conquest or challenge. Gaming addicts must play for long periods of time in order to excel at the game. Online games, especially MMORPGs [massive multiuser online role-playing games] are persistent worlds. That is, like the real world, they continue to exist whether players are in them or not. Characters who log out of a world simply enter a state of suspended animation and reappear in the same place again [when] they log back in. No one freezes his games into a save state when they depart, the way they do in a traditional video game.

Like the real world, MMORPG characters can grow indefinitely, becoming stronger, smarter, and more powerful over time. In order for them to grow, they must dedicate significant amounts of time playing the game. In doing so, they acquire more knowledge, advancement, and strength in the

I can't go mousing now Dad, I'm playing
this new massively multi-user online role-playing game
called "Virtual Mouse Hunt"...

game. This propels gaming addicts to play for significant periods of time, justifying their need to stay online and play. Health problems or potential health problems pale in comparison to having the character grow.

Health Risks

Online gaming is an emotionally draining and time-consuming activity. To create more time for the computer, gaming addicts neglect sleep, diet, exercise, hobbies, and socializing. They let their own health go as they do not get the proper rest and nutrition they need. They may suffer a number of health problems from back strain, eye strain, carpel tunnel syndrome, and repetitive stress injury. As one gaming addict explained, "I stopped bathing. I didn't eat unless it was a quick snack I could eat in front of my computer. I lost weight. My skin was pasty and pale. I didn't shave or comb my hair. I did nothing. I looked so bad that my mother told me I looked more like a heroin addict."

MMORPGs are inherently social environments created by multiple users. A study conducted by the International Gaming Research Unit at Nottingham Trent University in the United Kingdom has examined the social interactions that occur both within and outside of MMORPGs. In one of the most comprehensive studies to date, the sample consisted of 912 self-selected MMORPG players from 45 countries. MMORPGs were found to be highly socially interactive environments providing the opportunity to create strong friendships and emotional relationships. The study demonstrated that the social interactions in online gaming form a considerable element in the enjoyment of playing. The study showed MMORPGs can be extremely social games, with high percentages of gamers making life-long friends and partners. It was concluded that virtual gaming may allow players to express themselves in ways they may not feel comfortable doing in real life because of their appearance, gender, sexuality, and/or age.

The Impact on Individuals and Relationships

As gaming addicts form an important support group with each other and form intimate bonds, the damage is often done to marriages and real-life relationships. Couples break up because the gaming addict neglects the relationship. Young people break up in high school or college. Married couples end in separation and divorce. Family stability is disrupted.

The gaming addict stops interacting, stops participating, and stops feeling that these real-life relationships are as important. These once-cherished family relationships and friendships only take time away from gaming friends. They only take time for being with the people that the gamer feels good about, creating the sense that real-life relationships are less fulfilling.

Gamers can join groups, guilds, lead battles, or win wars in a virtual fantasy world. A large part of gaming is about making social relationships. Gamers make friends with other gamers who help them learn the "ropes" of playing the game. Multi-user role-playing games often include interactive features and options such as chat rooms and places to virtually hangout with other gamers. The social aspect is a primary factor in many game addictions. Games often have trouble with social relationships and feel lonely as if they have never truly belonged. This feeling can be especially powerful among children and adolescents who haven't felt a sense of belonging in their real lives and often their only other friends are fellow gamers. Parents who try to put time limits on the game may find a child becomes angry, irrational, and even violent. Adolescents who cannot access the game experience a loss. They want to be on the game and miss playing the game. This feeling can become so intense that they become irritable, anxious, or depressed when they are forced to go without it. As their feelings intensify, they stop thinking rationally and begin to act out towards others, especially a parent or anyone who threatens taking the game away. . . .

The Intense Focus on Gaming

The addiction process begins with a preoccupation with gaming. Gamers will think about the game when offline and often fantasize about playing the game when they should be concentrating on other things. Instead of thinking about the paper that needs to be completed for school, or going to class, or studying at the library, the gamer becomes completely focused on playing the game. Gamers start to miss deadlines, neglect work or social activities as being online and playing the game becomes their main priority.

Some gamers spend days and nights online. They do not eat, sleep, or take a shower because of the game. They lie to family and friends about what they are really doing on the computer. Students tell their parents that they are doing their homework, spouses tell their family that they are using the computer for work, and friends will make up excuses for why they cannot go out—all to find more time to play the game.

As the addiction progress grows, gamers become less interested in hobbies or activities that they used to enjoy and become more fascinated with living inside the game. As one mother explained, "My son loved baseball and played Varsity on his high school team until he discovered X-Box Live. His grades plummeted after he discovered the game, but it wasn't until he quit the baseball team that I knew that something was seriously wrong. He loved baseball too much. He won a baseball scholarship for college and dreamed about playing professionally. Now, nothing else matters to him except the game."

Some gamers experience personality changes the more addicted they become. A once outgoing and social husband or wife becomes withdrawn from their friends and family only to spend more time alone in front of the computer. A normally happy son or daughter becomes withdrawn only to prefer making friends in the game as the people that were once important in real life become less important. If the gamer does have real-life friends, they are usually fellow gamers. In some cases, gamers are introverts and have problems making social connections in real life and turn to the game for companionship and acceptance. . . .

The Effect on Adolescents

Adolescence alone, regardless of the involvement in the Internet, is an extremely challenging and complex transition for young individuals. Exploring and attempting to discover one's identity as an adolescent can be an overwhelming stage in one's life. In the event that an adolescent is using online gaming as an escape, it is more than likely that many more obstacles will be encountered and as a result a teen will struggle with unmanageable physical and emotional consequences. Adolescents are a major target audience for gaming advertisers and appear to be the most at risk for developing an addiction to online games.

Peer pressure and environmental distresses are chief influences for an adolescent becoming involved with gaming. Friends are often gamers, and as discussed, family dynamics can play a role in the development of online gaming addiction. Furthermore, children of substance abusing parents are shown to have an increased risk of using gaming as means to cope with problems such as developmental issues, school problems, health problems, delinquency, sexual problems, mental issues, and family problems.

It is much harder for a teen to recover from gaming addiction, especially when the computer is often a necessary component of their home and school environments.

> "*Playing these games a lot does not necessarily imply addiction; it just means that you are really into the game and enjoy it and are trying to get better at it.*"

Online Game Playing Is Not Addictive

Peter Gray

In the following viewpoint, Peter Gray argues that people who frequently play online games are not necessarily addicted; the vast majority of these people are intelligent and rational, and they simply enjoy the challenge of playing online games. Gray further maintains that any brain imaging studies that indicate an addictive nature to online game playing have been misrepresented. Peter Gray is a research professor at Boston College and the author of the books, Free to Learn *and* Psychology, *a college textbook now in its 6th edition.*

As you read, consider the following questions:

1. According to Peter Gray, does playing video games generally lead to being isolated from peers?

Peter Gray, "Video Game Addiction: Does It Occur? If So, Why?," *Psychology Today Blog*, February 2, 2012. http://www.psychologytoday.com/blog/freedom-learn. Copyright © 2012 by Peter Gray. All rights reserved. Reproduced by permission.

2. Most researchers who support the concept of video game addiction often compare it to what other behavioral addiction, according to Gray?

3. Has video game addiction been added to the official list of psychological disorders by the American Psychiatric Association, according to the Gray?

"Experts," especially those quoted frequently by the media, are constantly warning us of dangers to our kids. What usually grabs our attention and instills fear in our hearts are the case stories they present. Some child, somewhere, was out playing without a parent nearby and was abducted and murdered. Therefore, anyone who allows his or her child to play outside, not closely watched by an adult, is a negligent parent. Some distraught young man in South Korea plays a video game for fifty straight hours without stopping to sleep or eat, goes into cardiac arrest, and dies. Therefore, video games are addictive, dangerous, and we must either ban them or curtail their use so our children don't die like that poor South Korean.

The Distorted Dangers of Video Games

Case stories like these are tragic; and, yes, tragedies do happen, usually in ways that are completely unpredictable.... The fear-mongering "experts" and media will never run out of shocking stories to tell us.

Today, worldwide, hundreds of millions of people play video games. The vast majority of those players are perfectly normal people, meaning that nothing newsworthy ever happens to them, but some small percentage of them are killers, some are extraordinarily depressed, some are suicidal; and every day some video gamer somewhere does something terrible or experiences something terrible. All this is also true of the hundreds of millions of people who don't play video games. This is why case stories, by themselves, are worthless. If we want to know about the consequences of playing video games, or of anything else, we need well-designed research studies and statistics. The emphasis here is on the *well-designed*.

For many years now, researchers have been trying to prove that video games are bad. Much of the attention has focused on the violent content of some of the games, and many dozens of studies have been done in attempts to prove that playing violent video games causes real-world violence. This past year [2011], the US Supreme Court was faced with the task of evaluating that research, in the case of *Brown versus Entertainment Merchants Association*. After much testimony and study, the court concluded, "Studies purporting to show a connection between exposure to violent video games and harmful effects on children do not prove that such exposure causes minors to act aggressively." In 2010, the Australian government—faced with petitions to ban or restrict video games with violent content—reached a similar conclusion after evaluating all of the evidence. And social scientists who have scrutinized the studies and conducted meta-analyses of them have also come to that conclusion. . . .

Far from being isolating, video games generally draw young people together and help them learn to get along with one another. Far from being cognitively stultifying, video games—especially the newer, online multiplayer games—are extraordinarily challenging to players' mental powers and promote cognitive development. Now, however, I want to take on the question of "video game addiction." Next to claims about violence, claims about addiction have accounted for most of the bad press that video games have received.

A Flawed Analogy

Addiction is a word that is used in a variety of ways, but generally it refers to a compulsive (hard-to-resist) drive to take some substance or engage in some activity that is clearly not good for us and may even be ruining our lives. The clearest examples of addiction, of course, are chemical addictions, where people become physiologically dependent on some chemical—such as alcohol, nicotine, or heroin—and experience painful or debilitating withdrawal symptoms without it. But increasingly, and with some good reason, psychologists have begun to apply the term *addiction* to harmful behaviors that seem to become compulsive even though no chemical is consumed. Perhaps the best example of this is addictive gambling.

Many people suffer—and their families do too—because they can't seem to stop gambling. They gamble away all of their money, and then they borrow and gamble more and go deeply into debt; and then, when they can't borrow any more, they might steal and gamble that away, too, in a desperate, doomed attempt to get out of debt and save themselves and their families from ruin. People who feel compelled to gamble may do it because they see no other possible route out of their debts and/or because of the thrill that comes whenever they win, which motivates them to seek that thrill again. Compulsive gambling is a very serious and prevalent problem, although this hasn't prevented state legislatures from promoting gambling (in the form of casinos as well as state lotteries) in order to add to state coffers and reduce the taxes that non-gamblers have to pay.

Many if not most researchers who support the concept of video game addiction draw an analogy between video game playing and gambling. In fact, much of the research purporting to assess the prevalence of video game addiction . . . has employed the same questionnaire that is used to assess the prevalence of gambling addiction, changing only the word "gambling" to "video gaming." The analogy may be tempting to people who don't know much about video gaming. From a distance, playing a video game looks a little like gambling at a video screen in a casino. But think of the differences!

First of all, most gambling games—especially the ones that people become addicted to—are pure games of chance (for all except the very few who figure out some way to cheat). They are rigged in such a way that over the long run you will always lose, but in the short run you will sometimes win. There is excellent research indicating that the random, unpredictable nature of these rewards operates on the brains of some people to promote behavior that might reasonably be called addictive. The irrational "thinking" that accompanies the behavior and cannot be refuted is this: "The very next time I pull the lever I could hit the jackpot, so I'll pull it one more time."... and then one more time, and one more time, and one more time, and so on.

Games of Play—Not of Addiction

In contrast, video games are games of skill. They are like chess or any other game in which success depends on perseverance, intelligence, practice, and learning, not chance. The rewards are not random; they are earned. To move up to the next level you have to work hard. Moreover, the rewards in video games, as in chess, are purely in-game rewards (unless you are competing in a tournament for prize money). They are rewarding only because they signal mastery. Winning in these games doesn't produce real-world riches; and, more to the point, failing in these games doesn't lead to debt. This is why video games and chess are truly play, while gambling is not.

It's hard to imagine why anyone with a grain of intelligence would spend lots of time gambling unless something irrational was driving him or her to it. Considered as a game, gambling is just dumb. It requires no skill or intelligence whatsoever. You just keep doing the same stupid thing over and over again and sometimes you win and usually you don't. There's no legitimate sense of mastery. I can imagine some healthy people—who have extra cash to throw away and can't think of anything better to do with it—gambling occasionally, just as a lark; but to spend hours a week at gambling is almost by definition pathological. So, it is reasonable to posit that otherwise intelligent people who spend lots of time gambling must have some sort of irrational compulsion to do it, for which the term "addiction" may be an appropriate label.

Not so for video games or chess or other games that depend on skill and knowledge. The more you play these the more skill and knowledge you gain and the better you get at the game (and at anything else that uses similar skills or knowledge). You learn from your mistakes, and the more you play the better you get. So, playing these games a lot does not necessarily imply addiction; it just means that you are really into the game and enjoy it and are trying to get better at it. If you don't think that video gaming involves knowledge and intelligence, take a look at the online compendium of information associated with just one game, *World of Warcraft—WoW-wiki*. It's the second largest compendium of knowledge that can be found online! The first largest is Wikipedia. (I thank my colleague Mike Langlois for this bit of information.)

Misguided Claims of Brain Research

Some researchers who should know better have based their claim for the addictive nature of video gaming on brain research. If you do a little tooling around the *Psychology Today* blogs, you will find that one or more of my fellow bloggers are among those who have made this claim. Yes, indeed, functional brain imaging studies have shown that certain so-called "pleasure pathways" in the brain light up when gamblers hit the jackpot, and these same pathways also light up when video gamers achieve some goal within the game. Well, of course they do! If they didn't, that would just mean that hitting the jackpot or achieving success in a game isn't pleasurable. Everything that is pleasurable is pleasurable because of activity in pleasure centers of the brain.

I'm sure that if I were hooked up to an fMRI [functional magnetic resonance imaging] scanner my pleasure centers would light up every time I played a seven-letter word in Scrabble, or every time I got a favorable review on something I wrote, or every time I took a bite of pistachio ice cream, or every time my wife gave me the right kind of kiss. If we were to define every activity that activates the brain's "pleasure centers" as addictive, and therefore to be curtailed, we would have to curtail everything that's fun. We'd have to become Puritans, but then some of us might discover that our very success at Puritanism caused pleasure centers to light up, and then where would we be! Hey, what's the purpose of life anyway? Our national founding fathers perhaps betrayed their puritanical background when they declared that "pursuit of happiness" is a basic human right. Now we've got neuroscientists saying, "If it lights up the pleasure centers, beware of it!" Especially if it does so in kids.

The teams of psychologists and psychiatrists who create the official list of psychological disorders for the *Diagnostic and Statistical Manual* (DSM) of the American Psychiatric Association, after careful study, decided to add *gambling addiction* to the next edition of the manual, but decided not to add *video game addiction*, despite much pressure from practitioners who would like a new disorder to treat. I think they made the right decision in both cases. . . .

A Time Management Problem

Still, of course, some people let their dedication to video gaming—or to chess, or to skiing, or to anything else—interfere with other aspects of their life, and that can be a problem. Lots of us need to learn time management, especially as we reach adulthood, in order to do what we want to do and still fulfill our obligations to others. My loved ones sometimes remind me that it's not fair for me to spend *all* of my time reading and writing or going off alone bicycling or skiing.

But, let's not stigmatize any of this by calling it an addiction. Let's just call it a time management problem and figure out constructive ways to deal with it. . . .

In some cases people engage in an activity not just because of their enjoyment of it, but also because it is an escape from something painful in their lives or is the only route available to them to satisfy basic psychological needs. This can occur for adults as well as children. The activity that seems to become obsessive might be video gaming, or it might be something else.

Gaming as a Means of Coping

For instance, some adults devote far more time to their careers than they otherwise might, because that allows them to avoid an unpleasant family environment. Some kids say they play video games at least partly as a means of escape, and some say they do so because it is the only realm of activity in which they feel free. In an age in which children are often not allowed to play freely outdoors, and in which they are more or less constantly directed by adults, the virtual world of video games is for some the only realm where they are allowed to roam free and explore. If they were allowed more autonomy in the real world, many of them would spend less time at video games.

As illustration of this idea, British gaming researcher Richard Wood gives some case examples. One case is that of Martin, an 11-year-old boy whose mother became concerned about the huge amounts of time he was devoting to *World of Warcraft* and therefore forbade him from playing it or other video games, which made things only worse for Martin. It turned out, according to Wood, that Martin was an only child who was being bullied at school and hated going there, and who was afraid of going outside at home because of repeated bullying. The online video game was his only source of free expression and his only satisfying contact with other people. When this was taken away from him, he was understandably distraught. . . .

In a study of more than 1,300 adult video gamers (age 18 to 43), Andrew Przybylski and his colleagues at the University of Rochester found that a small percentage of them, who played many hours per day, described themselves as obsessively engaged—they felt that they didn't just "want" to play, but "needed" to play. These players, when they stopped a session of playing, did not feel refreshed and energized as other players did, but felt tense and unhappy. The extensive questionnaires used in this study also revealed that these "obsessed" players were, in general, those whose basic psychological needs—their needs for freedom, competence, and social relationships—were not being met in real life.

So, if your child or another loved one seems obsessed about video games and unhappy outside of the games, don't jump to the conclusion that the games are cause of the unhappiness. Instead, talk with your loved one and try to find out what might be missing or wrong in other aspects of his or her life and whether or not you can help to solve that problem.

Periodical and Internet Sources Bibliography

The following articles have been selected to supplement the diverse views presented in this chapter.

Nicholas Grant Boeving	"Is Addiction Really a Disease? A Challenge to Twelve-Step Programs," *Tikkun*, vol. 26, no. 4, Fall 2011.
Robert DuPont and Andrea Barthwell	"Don't Legalize Marijuana. It's Addictive," *Seattle Times*, October 1, 2012.
Jan Goldsmith	"Legalizing Medical Marijuana Properly," *U-T San Diego*, October 11, 2012.
Cecile LaBore	"Addictive Disease: Why Semantics Matter—and Why They Don't," Recovery Systems Institute, May 28, 2012.
Marc Lewis	"A Brain's-Eye View of Addiction as a 'Disease'," *Psychology Today*, June 27, 2012.
Lisa Miller	"Hooked on a Feeling: The Dangers of Behavioral Addictions," ABCNews, October 13, 2012.
Pat O'Connor	"The Fallacy of the 'Hijacked Brain'," *New York Times*, June 10, 2012.
Nancy Paull	"Community Voices: Debating the Definition of Addiction," *Herald News*, June 22, 2012.
Ronald Pies	"Should DSM-V Designate 'Internet Addiction' a Mental Disorder?" *Psychiatry*, February 2009.
Stanton E. Samenow	"An Alternative View of 'Compulsive' Gambling," *Psychology Today*, September 5, 2011.
Carolyn Sun	"Online Cravings," *Newsweek*, October 17, 2011.
Ian Urbina	"Addiction Diagnoses May Rise Under Guideline Changes," *New York Times*, May 11, 2012.

OPPOSING VIEWPOINTS® SERIES

CHAPTER 2

How Can Addiction Be Prevented?

Chapter Preface

In the United States today, approximately 80 million people, ages twelve and older, engage in hazardous substance use. According to the 2010 *National Survey on Drug Use and Health*, young adults between the ages of eighteen and twenty-five have the highest rates of substance use and dependence. And a study published in the April 2012 issue of *Archives of General Psychiatry* found that 78 percent of teens have abused alcohol and over 40 percent have used other drugs. According to the American Academy of Child and Adolescent Psychiatry, the average age of people who use marijuana for the first time is fourteen, and alcoholic use can begin as early as twelve. These statistics seem daunting, but research also shows that it is possible to substantially reduce the risk of substance use in teens. It begins with parents.

While peer pressure is a strong factor in teen drug use, parents may be surprised to learn that they are extremely influential with their children when it comes to drug and alcohol use. In fact, parents are the most important influence, according to the National Center on Addiction and Substance Abuse at Columbia University (CASAColumbia). In its June 2011 report, *Adolescent Substance Use: America's #1 Public Health Problem*, CASAColumbia writes, "A significant body of evidence shows that a positive family environment and positive parenting practices related to affection, support, monitoring, rules, discipline, and reward are associated with reduced risk of teen substance use." The report also states, "Parents' involvement helps more than anything else. . . . Good influences at home are the best prevention."

Teens who do not have a close relationship with their parents or who receive little parental supervision, however, have an increased risk of addiction. According to the report *National Survey of American Attitudes on Substance Abuse XV:*

Teens and Parents, published in 2010 by CasaColumbia, teens in families with weak family ties are four times more likely to have tried tobacco, almost three times more likely to have tried alcohol, and four times more likely to have tried marijuana than teens who have strong family ties. Furthermore, parents who themselves engage in substance use behaviors, such as abusing prescription drugs or drinking alcohol on a regular basis, put their children at a high risk of substance use and addiction. In his book, *When Things Get Crazy with Your Teen: The Why, the How, and What to Do Now*, psychologist Michael Bradley writes, "Parental modeling is the most powerful way to shape a child's values (and thus her behavior). . . . The only people in America indulging in more irresponsible behaviors than the teens are the *adults*." Husband and wife psychoanalysts Morteza Khaleghi and Karen Khaleghi agree with Bradley's view. In their book, *The Anatomy of Addiction: Overcoming the Triggers That Stand in the Way of Recovery*, they write, "A parent is both a guardian and a guide—the driver of the family car, so to speak; when the person who is driving the car takes a wrong turn on the wrong road, it is almost impossible to expect that the child will end up at a different destination."

Research consistently shows that strong family bonds and proactive parenting play a critical role in preventing substance abuse among adolescents. Educating parents about the important influence their own attitudes and behaviors have on their children is vital in raising children to be addiction free. As Bradley puts it: "So, for better or for worse, our teenagers are very much a reflection of *who we adults are*, not what kind of adults we tell our children to become."

| "Screening for risky use of addictive substances is comparable to offering regularly scheduled pap smears or colonoscopies to identify cancer indicators."

Screening and Early Intervention Help Prevent Teen Substance Use and Addiction

The National Center on Addiction and Substance Abuse at Columbia University (CASA Columbia)

The National Center on Addiction and Substance Abuse at Columbia University (CASA Columbia) strives to educate the public on the economic and social costs of substance use and addiction and to provide health care providers, policymakers, and individuals with the tools necessary for the prevention and treatment of addiction. In the following viewpoint, CASA Columbia maintains that screening and early intervention services are invaluable tools in the prevention of substance use and addiction,

The National Center on Addiction and Substance Abuse at Columbia University (CASA Columbia), "Chapter IV: Screening and Early Intervention," *Addiction Medicine: Closing the Gap between Science and Practice*, The National Center on Addiction and Substance Abuse at Columbia University (CASA Columbia), June 2012, pp. 63–67, 69, 71, 74–79. http://www.casacolumbia.org/templates/Publications_Reports.aspx#r116. This version is excerpted from the original and all footnotes and citations have been omitted. Reproduced by permission.

especially among adolescents and young people. CASA Columbia further contends that studies have proven the effectiveness of screening and brief interventions in reducing the risky use of tobacco, alcohol, and illicit drugs and the misuse of prescription drugs in people of all ages. This version of the text is excerpted from the original and all footnotes and citations have been omitted.

As you read, consider the following questions:

1. According to CASA Columbia, what is the most critical period for the onset of substance abuse?

2. Are confrontational interventions equally effective as those offering sympathy and encouragement, according to the author?

3. Are school health programs effective in screening for people at risk, according to the author?

Nearly one-third (31.7 percent) of the U.S. population (80.4 million people ages 12 and older) engages in substance use that threatens their own health or safety or the health and safety of others, but does not meet clinical diagnostic criteria for addiction. Few of these individuals, however, are routinely screened for risky use of addictive substances or receive any services designed to reduce such use such as brief interventions. Of those who do receive some form of screening, in most cases it involves only one type of substance use—tobacco or alcohol—which fails to identify risky use of other substances or recognize that 30.6 percent of risky users who are not addicted engage in risky use of more than one substance. . . .

For many health conditions, certain developmental periods are associated with increased risk of acquiring a disease. Addiction, in most cases, has its roots in adolescence with the initiation of risky use of addictive substances, but the onset of risky use and addiction can occur at any point in the lifespan.

Each life phase presents unique vulnerabilities that must be recognized, as well as the basic risk factors that may be present at any time in life.

The Need for Screening During Childhood and Adolescence

Adolescence is *the* critical period for the onset of substance use and its consequences, but signs of risk sometimes can be observed much earlier. In addition to the overall risks associated with substance use, children and adolescents with heightened risk of engaging in substance use, of experiencing the adverse consequences of risky use and of developing addiction include:

- Those with certain genetic predispositions or structural or functional brain characteristics that make them more susceptible to addictive substances;

- Young children whose temperaments' are more active, impatient, aggressive and nonconforming than their peers,

- Those with behavioral disorders including oppositional defiant disorder and conduct disorder, those who engage in bullying and those who have sleep problems; and

- Children who are maltreated, abused or have suffered other trauma.

As children age, moving through elementary and middle school—a period that coincides with first-time exposure to cigarettes and other drugs—they are presented with increasing academic and social challenges and responsibilities that increase their risk of trying addictive substances and engaging in substance use.

During adolescence and into early adulthood the brain undergoes considerable developmental changes, explaining why adolescence is such a risky period for the onset of substance use and addiction. Hormonal changes that occur during adolescence also pose a biological risk for substance use in this age group. The surge in the female hormone estrogen and the male hormone testosterone during puberty is associated with risk taking and sensation seeking. The lack of fully developed decision-making and impulse-control skills combined with the hormonal changes of puberty compromise an adolescent's ability to assess risks and make them uniquely vulnerable to substance use.

Other psychological and social challenges faced by adolescents—such as the struggle to develop a sense of identity, feeling less satisfied with one's appearance and experiencing peer pressure to conform—contribute to the risk.

The Need for Screening During Young Adulthood

In recent years, researchers have begun to recognize the developmental stage of young adulthood—often referred to as emerging adulthood—as a period of life that is strongly associated with risky use. Young adults facing heightened risk include:

- College students—while approximately two-thirds of college students who engage in substance use began to smoke, drink or use other drugs in high school or earlier, the culture on many college campuses permits and promotes risky use rather than curtailing it.

- Young adults facing work-related stress or instability in living arrangements, social relations or academic or career choices. As marriage and parenthood have become delayed, the phase of life devoted to academics and career development has stretched well into the twenties. Young adults may turn to addictive substances to relieve these forms of stress and self-medicate their anxiety and emotional troubles. . . .

Attending to Co-occurring Conditions

Individuals who engage in risky use or who have addiction frequently suffer from other co-occurring health conditions. Therefore, any attempt to identify risky use of addictive substances, evaluate an individual's risk for developing addiction or assess a substance user's need for intervention or treatment must involve identification of co-occurring conditions and plans to address them. Being informed of a patient's health conditions that might be caused or exacerbated by substance use or that might cause or exacerbate the patient's addiction will help medical professionals determine appropriate interventions and provide effective care. Similarly, medical professionals treating patients with medical conditions that frequently co-occur with risky use and addiction—such as hypertension, gastritis and injuries—should be prompted to screen for risky use of addictive substances that may cause or aggravate these conditions.

Patient Education and Motivation

Educating patients and motivating them to reduce their risky use of addictive substances is a critical component of preventive care. As part of routine medical practice, medical and other health professionals should educate their patients (and parents of young patients) about:

1. The adverse consequences of risky use and the nature of addiction—that it is a disease that can be prevented and treated effectively;

2. The risk factors for substance use, tailoring the information to the patient's age, gender, mental health history and other relevant medical, social and demographic characteristics;

3. Times of increased risk for substance use, such as adolescence, key life transitions and stressful life experiences; and

4. Steps patients can take to prevent risky use of addictive substances and the onset of addiction, e.g., by delaying initiation of substance use, following guidelines for the safe use of alcohol and of controlled prescription medications, being vigilant for signs and symptoms of risk and seeking professional help at the first sign of trouble.

The Use of Screening

Screening, a staple of public health practice that dates back to the 1930s, serves to identify early signs of risk for or evidence of a disease or other health condition and distinguish between individuals who require minimal intervention and those who may need more extended treatment. It is an effective method of preventive care in many medical specialties, and risky use of addictive substances is no exception. Screening for risky use of addictive substances is comparable to offering regularly scheduled pap smears or colonoscopies to identify cancer indicators.

Screening tools typically are brief and easy to administer and are to be implemented with a relatively broad population to identify indications of risk involving smoking, drinking or using other drugs. Screening tools typically include written or oral questionnaires and, less frequently, clinical and laboratory tests. . . .

Brief Interventions and Treatment Referrals

For those who screen positive for risky use of addictive substances that does not meet the threshold of clinical addiction, providing brief interventions is an effective, low-cost approach to reducing risky use.

Brief interventions generally include feedback about the extent and effects of patients' substance use and recommendations for how they might change their behavior. Brief interventions often involve motivational interviewing techniques and substance-related education; the exact approach may differ depending on the target population. Brief interventions can be conducted face-to-face, over the phone or via computerized feedback to patients. They can be performed by health professionals after relatively limited training. Providing brief interventions can save lives and reduce a broad range of negative health and social consequences including addiction.

For individuals showing signs of addiction, providing treatment or referral to specialty care is critical to managing the condition and preventing further health and social consequences. . . .

Helping patients understand how they can change their behavior and encouraging them to be optimistic about their ability to do so are important components of most brief interventions. Interventions delivered in an empathetic counseling style are more effective than those that rely on confrontation or coercion. While brief interventions can avert the development of a more serious substance use problem, individuals with the disease of addiction require more intensive care and should be treated or referred to specialty care.

The combination of screening and brief interventions has shown positive results for tobacco, alcohol, illicit drugs and the misuse of controlled prescription drugs, across many settings and population groups.

Several large-scale studies have explored the effectiveness of screening and brief interventions in reducing the consumption of addictive substances as well as the serious problems and costs that accompany such behavior, including visits to emergency departments, hospitalization, high-risk injection drug use, criminal activity, psychiatric stress and depression. One study found that adult patients receiving a brief intervention after a positive screen by their primary care physicians for risky alcohol use experienced 20 percent fewer emergency department visits and 37 percent fewer days of hospitalization than patients who did not receive the intervention. Participants who received screening and brief interventions also had significantly fewer arrests for alcohol or controlled drug violations (two vs. 11 arrests). . . .

Implementing Screening and Brief Interventions in Health Care Settings

While screening and brief interventions can be provided in a broad range of venues, health care settings may be the most effective. Physicians and other health care providers, including dental professionals, nurses and pharmacists, typically are a consistent, trusted and influential presence in the lives of children and adults and their professional position grants them the authority and credibility to deliver effective, evidence-based interventions to patients at risk for complications related to their substance use, including addiction. Part of the success of incorporating these services for risky use of addictive substances into standard medical practice is that people tend to be more receptive to health messages once they are in a health care setting. Patients view additional screening, information, brief intervention or referral to treatment as part of the health care they sought initially. The use of technology to assist in the completion of screening and brief interventions holds promise for helping to integrate these practices into routine health care delivery. . . .

Screening the adolescent population for substance use may be the single most effective preventive step that can be taken to address the problem of risky use and addiction in this country since the consequences of risky use of addictive substances among adolescents are so profound and individuals with addiction typically began engaging in risky use in adolescence.

The U.S. Public Health Service's clinical practice guideline for tobacco use and dependence recommends that clinicians ask adolescent patients about their tobacco use and provide them with brief interventions to aid in quitting.

Professional medical associations such as the American Medical Association (AMA) and the American Academy of Pediatrics (AAP) support screening adolescent patients for substance use, and promote the use of screening and brief intervention techniques among their constituents. . . .

Implementing Screening and Brief Interventions in High School, College and University Settings

Screening and brief intervention programs reduce risky use of addictive substances among students by changing their attitudes, beliefs and expectations regarding tobacco, alcohol and other drug use.

School health programs, in collaboration with primary care providers, are important opportunities for screening adolescents and young adults for substance use, primarily because young people spend a majority of their time in school. Few schools, however, take advantage of this opportunity. . . .

The college setting also is ideal for intervening with young people at risk via screening and brief interventions because of the high rates of substance use in the college population; an estimated 67.2 percent are risky users or have addiction. To date, the majority of the screening- and intervention-related research among college students has focused on alcohol, most likely because alcohol typically is the substance most likely to be used by college students. Screening and brief interventions have proven successful in reducing risky alcohol use and its consequences in this population. The Department of Education recommends the implementation of screening and brief intervention programs in all college health centers.

> *"Schools would do well to recognize that empirical research has failed to demonstrate deterrent effects and that commentators have raised myriad, and often serious, potential downsides to the testing."*

Drug Testing Is Ineffective in Preventing Teen Substance Abuse and Addiction

Frank Butler

In the following viewpoint, Frank Butler asserts that deterring adolescents from abusing drugs and alcohol is a commendable goal for public schools; however, drug testing students is not an effective or ethical solution. Butler maintains that studies of random drug testing programs show disappointing results, and in some cases drug testing studies actually show an increased risk for future substance abuse. Frank Butler has a JD and a PhD in criminal justice; his research interests include criminal law, juvenile justice, and social ethics.

As you read, consider the following questions:

1. According to Frank Butler, has the use of cigarettes and alcohol among secondary school students increased?

2. Is alcohol generally included in school drug testing programs, according to Butler?

3. According to Butler, do school drug testing programs usually survive search and seizure challenges regarding constitutional freedoms?

Discouraging adolescents from ingesting harmful, psychoactive substances is a relevant goal for public schools. Also, encouraging those same students to value constitutional freedoms is an enduring understanding for the schools to cultivate. The two purposes, however, exist in tension when schools adopt programs of drug testing that are not based on individualized suspicion but rather on a general premise that at least some members of certain categories of students may be users of illicit drugs. This essay reviews the legal and social issues involved in such testing and includes an analysis of the socio-ethico-legal challenges the testing entails.

Substance Abuse Among Students

Though use of cigarettes and alcohol among secondary-school students is at its lowest level in at least 35 years, relatively high rates of abuse of marijuana, prescription drugs, and non-cigarette tobacco products (e.g., hookahs, smokeless tobacco) remain. For example, nearly 22 percent of 12th-graders report binge drinking (five or more drinks in a row over the past two weeks), 11 percent report using synthetic marijuana ("Spice"), 8 percent abuse the opioid painkiller Vicodin, and 8 percent abuse amphetamines.

Substance abuse in adolescence increases risks of deleterious behaviors at that stage of development and well into adulthood. Examples of behaviors that have been correlated with substance abuse include: impaired driving, interpersonal violence, poor academic performance, disturbed family and interpersonal relationships, and criminal activity.

The Trend Toward Random Drug Testing

Drug testing of students generally increased in the early 21st century, with approximately 25 percent of districts with a middle- and/or high-school having a student drug-testing policy, and 56 percent of those districts (or 14 percent of districts overall) including random testing in their policies. [According to an article in a 2008 issue of *American Journal of Public Health*,] more than one-quarter of districts with random testing subjected all students to it, a practice that is more encompassing than the protocol approved by the U.S. Supreme Court in 2002. As technology enables testing of less "intrusive" samples than urine (e.g., hair, saliva), legal privacy concerns may be further diminished, with consequent court-approved expansions in testing. . . .

Disappointing Results of Drug-Testing Trials

Results of empirical studies of random drug testing generally show disappointing results in terms of deterrent effect. For example, . . . national survey data of eighth-, tenth-, and twelfth-grade students [found] that among high-school male athletes, use of illicit drugs showed no significant difference between schools with and without drug testing. Also, among all students surveyed, "school drug testing was not associated with either the prevalence or the frequency of student marijuana use, or of other illicit drug use."

A prospective randomized control trial of drug testing of student-athletes was undertaken at eleven Oregon high schools. . . . The [schools were] divided . . . into a control group without drug testing and an experimental group that initiated drug testing at the start of the study. Over the course of two years, the testing schools showed significantly lower mean past-year drug use (measured by student-athlete self-report surveys), compared to the non-testing schools, but those results existed for only two of four follow-up time periods. Also, past-month drug use (where testing would be expected to have its greatest deterrent effect) showed no difference between control and experimental groups at any of the four follow-up time periods over two years. Finally, somewhat paradoxically, over time, athletes in the testing schools "had less belief in their athletic competence, believed less in the benefits of testing, believed that authorities were less opposed to drug use, and believed less that testing was not a reason to use drugs." All of those attitudes would seem to represent increased risk for future substance abuse. . . .

Students' Opinions About Drug Testing

[In 2005] middle- and high-school students [were surveyed] in four schools, representing grades 6 through 12. Nearly 45 percent of respondents said they had experimented with drugs, and nearly 75 percent said they had used alcohol. None of the schools had a drug-testing program. Most students said they would still participate in after-school activities if drug testing was required, but most students also felt that drug testing would violate their privacy. Students who reported frequent use of drugs or alcohol were least apt to believe drug testing would control drug use among students. Frequent drug use was significantly less common among students who participated in after-school activities (11 percent) than among those who did not (19 percent). In contrast, frequent alcohol use did not differ significantly between the two groups. . . .

[In 2006 students were surveyed] at two rural high schools that were about to implement an aggressive program of drug testing. The testing would involve alcohol, tobacco, and illicit drugs, and it would involve any student in grade 6 through 12 who participated in any extracurricular activity or was issued a school parking permit. Though three-quarters of respondents believed the new policy would reduce drug use, 40 percent of respondents thought that the consequences of testing positive would be nothing or minimal. . . .

Addressing Steroids

The use of anabolic steroids and other performance enhancing supplements by professional athletes has prompted legislators and other policymakers to address steroid use among adolescents. On the surface, random drug testing appears to be a viable, effective deterrent to many. Research, however, does not support this approach. As with other forms of drug testing, those targeting steroids have not proven to be an effective means of reducing use. Further, steroid testing impairs the relationship of trust between students, parents, coaches and other school administrators. . . .

Most steroid tests do not detect other performance enhancing supplements, and the more substances that are added to a test, the higher the cost. Also, testing does not reach all of those adolescents who are using steroids, as more than one-third of adolescent users do not participate in school sports. For those who do participate in sports, testing is a poor substitute for learning and appreciating the value of fair play.

Jennifer Kern, Fatema Gunja, Alexandra Cox,
Marsha Rosenbaum, Judith Appel, and Anjuli Verma,
Making Sense of Student Drug Testing:
Why Educators Are Saying No. Santa Cruz, CA:
American Civil Liberties Union, January 2006.

Inconsistencies in Drug-Testing Programs

A mail survey and interviews with high-school principals [found] that most schools without random drug testing did not consider instituting it in the aftermath of the *Earls* decision [US Supreme Court decision in *Board of Education of Indep. School Dist. No. 92 of Pottawatomie County v. Earls* in which the Court upheld the constitutionality of mandatory drug testing of students participating in extracurricular activities by public schools]. Schools with high rates of parental contact, high standardized test scores, low truancy rates, and high instructional expenditures per pupil generally did not use random drug testing, nor did schools that scored low on those variables. . . . In wealthy districts, strong parental influence likely inhibits testing programs, as influential parents do not wish their children to undergo testing that may have adverse ramifications. On the other hand, in poor schools, there is probably insufficient political energy to start random testing. It is in middle-range schools, where parents have less time to be involved in policy-making, that political power to start a program of random testing may devolve to principals, though "principals are making policy in the absence of data to show that random drug testing actually deters student drug use."

In a [2009] survey of state-level education agencies and a sample of school districts, . . . both gave low priority to student drug testing. This is in spite of the fact that both the U.S. Department of Education and the U.S. Office of National Drug Control Policy have made drug testing a high-priority strategy. In another survey of school districts, . . . nearly half of respondent school districts notified law enforcement of positive results from drug testing (including a first positive test), thereby potentially violating the federal Family Education Rights and Privacy Act (FERPA) and the federal Confidentiality of Alcohol and Drug Abuse Patient Records. Other punitive responses included: one-third of districts with drug testing suspended students who tested positive, 13 percent sent such students to alternative schools, and 8 percent expelled the students. . . .

A More Effective Approach

The general trend countenancing more expansive, non-individualized drug-testing of students seems on a collision course with public-health approaches, which focus on harm reduction and which counsel great caution with regard to widespread drug testing. Though legally (i.e., with regard to the U.S. and many state constitutions) such testing usually survives "search and seizure" challenges, schools would do well to recognize that empirical research has failed to demonstrate deterrent effects and that commentators have raised myriad, and often serious, potential downsides to the testing.

A school environment that is non-threatening and in which students are provided with realistic tools for understanding and dealing with the diverse social pressures they face may be a more effective goal than an admittedly more expedient program of random drug testing, if schools are meaningfully to influence students' worlds regarding drugs. Such an environment would cultivate an earned sense of trust that students can feel with adults, especially at school. The school would value a holistic approach to drug abuse, addressing not only students but also the families and communities that are so integral to their everyday lives. In the long run such a perspective may be far more effective in changing drug-related behaviors than a "gotcha" approach that ascribes guilt only to those who "randomly" get caught.

> *"Knowledge about dangers is certainly a factor in prevention, and youth need to receive this message from both school and home, but that's only one piece of the puzzle."*

Many School Drug Prevention Programs Are Ineffective

Celine Provini

In the following viewpoint, Celine Provini contends that many school-based drug prevention programs are ineffective in curbing substance abuse and that telling youth that drugs are dangerous and should be avoided is simply not enough to change behavior. Provini further suggests that administering youth surveys to ascertain students' attitudes and promoting healthy alternatives to risky behavior would be more beneficial. Celine Provini is the author of the book, A Parent's Guide to Preventing Underage Drinking *and the editor of EducationWorld, a website where teachers gather and share high-quality lesson plans and research material.*

As you read, consider the following questions:

1. Because research suggests that it is important to have clear and consistently enforced no-drug-use policies, is zero tolerance an effective policy, according to Celine Provini?

2. According to Provini, do presentations by law enforcement have a significant impact on students' drug use?

3. According to Provini, "risk behaviors" surveys are important tools in student drug prevention. What is an appropriate question the survey should include?

Too many popular school-based substance-abuse prevention programs lack grounding in science, the *Los Angeles Times* reported back in 2006. The situation is probably not much different today [2011]. Past studies have shown that only 35 percent of public schools and 13 percent of private schools are implementing prevention programs with demonstrated effectiveness, despite the fact that No Child Left Behind [Act of 2001] requires schools receiving federal funding to use evidence-based programs.

Programs That Do Not Work

Time-honored but ineffective programs include one-time events, or presentations that simply explain the dangers of various substances (these can actually increase young people's interest in trying alcohol and drugs). Other common offenders include "scared straight" approaches that feature crashed-car displays, guest speakers in recovery from addiction, and people who've lost friends and relatives to drunk driving. Sure, kids will tell you these experiences were meaningful and that they liked them, but there's no evidence that liking a program or experiencing an "emotionally powerful" presentation leads to changes in youth behavior.

Similarly, trying to curb substance abuse with punitive "zero-tolerance" policies may work for the police, but is generally ineffective and counterproductive in a school setting. Research tells us that schools should have clear and consistently enforced no-[drug-]use policies, but should not suspend students without considering the context of the situation, providing support services and offering opportunities to re-connect to the school community. For example, see the report *Zero Tolerance, Zero Evidence* (Skiba, 2000). Here's another message that research sends loud and clear: Having law enforcement deliver classroom sessions is a wonderful tool for building youth-police relationships, but has little impact on kids' actual substance use. David Hanson's article "Drug Abuse Resistance Education: The Effectiveness of Dare" offers a review of research on this topic.

Information Alone Does Not Lead to Prevention

It's tempting to think that telling kids "drugs are dangerous and bad" will somehow convince them not to use. We often approach drug prevention with the same assumptions that underlie history or math class—if we give them the knowledge, they'll be able to apply it, or at least remember it on test day. The problem is that kids use alcohol, tobacco and other drugs based on a complex set of psychological and sociological motivations and influences. For some, using substances is viewed positively within youth culture and is also strongly linked to personal identity, the wish to feel like an independent adult, and the desire for social status among peers.

"Oversimplification is just one reason most school-based drug-prevention programs don't work," said researcher David Hanson, of the University of North Carolina at Chapel Hill, in the article "Popular prevention programs lack nuance, research." "The decisions kids face are more nuanced than most drug programs make them appear."

Knowledge about dangers is certainly a factor in prevention, and youth need to receive this message from both school and home, but that's only one piece of the puzzle. After all, isn't the danger of alcohol and drugs part of the reason they're so attractive to teens? Young people, feeling invincible, routinely underestimate risks. And don't we hear youth saying, after hearing of a case of serious harm from alcohol or drugs, "Yes, but that won't happen to *me?*" This is why "information" approaches aimed directly at kids are the least effective type of prevention strategy. Read more in Wakefield and Campain's tip sheet "Don't Do It! Ineffective Prevention Strategies."

Emphasis Should Be on Positive Behavior

So if one-time guest speakers, sad or scary stories, zero-tolerance policies and lectures about substance-abuse dangers aren't that effective, why do many schools continue to invest time and money in these strategies? Part of the confusion may be that these types of activities do help to raise general awareness, and also reinforce the behavior of kids who already plan to steer clear of substances. "Preaching to the choir" is not the same thing as prevention, however—prevention efforts should strive to lower the risk of harm within the youth population as a whole. For some youth this means getting them to avoid ever trying substances; for others this means helping them stop use, reduce use to a less dangerous level, or begin experimentation at a later age. In order to accomplish these goals, prevention approaches must try to counter the powerful social and cultural contexts that encourage kids to use alcohol and drugs.

Yes, it is possible to influence young people so that they are more likely to make the right choices. There are a few types of strategies that have been around a while, yet might be just the breath of fresh air that your school's alcohol, tobacco and other drug (ATOD) prevention efforts need. You'll notice that these ideas don't even really address substances—at least not via lectures or lesson plans—and that's the whole point. As Cindy Wakefield and James Campain, the authors of "Don't

Do It," note, "Our time and energy is best used to teach positive, healthy behavior, rather than fruitlessly trying to stop dangerous behavior through manipulation and punishment."

Remember that any strategy, effort or program in your school should be regularly evaluated to determine whether it is effective. Sometimes even "model programs" from federal registries can fall flat, especially if your school lacks the infrastructure for full-strength implementation, or if the program is not a good cultural match for your student population. At the very least, you will need to administer a youth "risk behaviors" survey annually or every other year to track changes in student substance use. (If your state already requires you to do this, you're in luck.) Among other things, survey questions should assess (1) past 30-day or past-year use of various substances, (2) the age at which student first used various substances, (3) whether students believe these substances are harmful, and (4) whether students believe parents and peers disapprove of use of these substances. One such survey is the Search Institute's *Profiles of Student Life: Attitudes and Behaviors.* . . .

Strategies That Have Been Proven Effective

1—Build "developmental assets" and student strengths/skills that are incompatible with substance use.

Developmental assets are strengths both internal and external to students that when present, markedly reduce the likelihood of a young person engaging in risky behaviors, including alcohol and drug use. Assets include things like experiencing a caring, encouraging school environment; having a useful role in the community; and spending three or more hours per week in sports, clubs, or organizations at school and/or in community organizations. There are many ways in which schools can help build assets—with no purchased programs, high-priced trainers or guest speakers required.

Zero Tolerance: The "School-to-Prison Pipeline"

Considering its origin and use over the years, zero tolerance can best be defined as a "philosophy or policy that mandates the application of predetermined consequences, most often severe and punitive in nature, that are intended to be applied regardless of the seriousness of behavior, mitigating circumstances, or situational context." The severity and punitive nature of zero tolerance practices escalated with the placement of police on school campus, resulting in a considerable increase in the number of students arrested and referred to juvenile court for infractions once handled by school administrators. The study of this occurrence has been referred to as the "school-to-prison pipeline."

Steven C. Teske,
"A Study of Zero Tolerance Policies in Schools:
A Multi-Integrated Systems Approach
to Improve Outcomes for Adolescents,"
Journal of Child and Adolescent Psychiatric Nursing,
vol. 24, no. 2, May 2011, p. 89.

Life Skills, a federal model program, is proven to reduce the risks of alcohol, tobacco, drug abuse, and violence by targeting the major social and psychological factors that promote the initiation of substance use. Rather than merely teaching information about the dangers of drug abuse, the program promotes healthy alternatives to risky behavior.

2—Make sure that every student is connected to at least one caring adult who serves as a positive role model.

Even when caring adults don't directly discuss substance use with youth, their emotional support and positive example can speak volumes. Schools can provide informal mentoring by pairing students up with staff members (even non-teaching staff can make excellent mentors). More formal youth mentoring programs, such as those that follow the national "Elements of Effective Practice" guidelines, are more intensive and can provide even greater benefit.

While you're at it, consider helping students make positive connections with each other—try mixing up cliques and providing structured interactions among groups of students who typically wouldn't connect.

3—Short-circuit typical peer norms so that students view avoidance of alcohol, tobacco and other drugs to be "cooler" than using these substances.

Social norms marketing can be applied within a school to help students develop accurate perceptions of levels of peer substance use. Since youth often overestimate levels of peer use, once students recognize that "not everyone is doing it," they will be less motivated to use substances themselves.

Rescue Social Change Group has developed an innovative method of social norms marketing that takes into account the unique influence of culture, youth identity and social environments on youth risk behaviors within a particular school community. The company uses "social branding" (a subtle approach that makes very little direct mention of substances and avoids preaching and scare tactics) to make substance-free lifestyles an appealing choice for students. Instead of "preaching to the choir," the approach actively engages higher-risk students who may be experimenting with substances, since these often-popular students are in the best position to market ideas to their peers.

> "*Effective drug education should be based on sound science and acknowledge teenagers' ability to understand, analyze and evaluate.*"

Reality-Based School Programs Help Prevent Teen Drug Use

Marsha Rosenbaum

In the following viewpoint, Marsha Rosenbaum maintains that drugs are an integral part of today's American culture; therefore, occasional experimentation with legal and illegal substances by young people should be expected. Rosenbaum further contends that because teenagers are savvy regarding the pervasiveness of drugs, the best drug prevention programs should incorporate honest education regarding the legal and physical consequences of drug use, how drugs affect the mind and body, and the importance of moderation. Marsha Rosenbaum is the director of the San Francisco, California, office of the Drug Policy Alliance, a national organization that promotes sensible drug policy reforms. She is also the author of the booklet, Just Say What?: An Alternative View on Solving America's Drug Problem.

As you read, consider the following questions:

1. According to Marsha Rosenbaum, is peer pressure a significant factor in teenage drug use?

2. Is it possible to do well academically while under the influence of alcohol and/or drugs, according to Rosenbaum?

3. According to Rosenbaum, are in-home, drug-testing kits recommended as a drug-prevention tool?

The 2010 Monitoring the Future survey states that more than 48 percent of high school seniors have tried illegal drugs at some point in their lifetime; 38 percent used a drug during the past year; and nearly 23.8 percent profess to have used drugs in the past month. The numbers are even higher for alcohol: 72.5 percent have tried alcohol (itself a potent drug in every regard); 65 percent have used it within the year; and 41 percent (almost twice the statistic for marijuana) of those surveyed imbibed "once a month or more." The Centers for Disease Control and Prevention's (CDC) 2009 Youth Risk Behavior Survey found that 21 percent of high school students reported taking "more than a few sips" of alcohol before the age of 13.

A Culture of Drug Use

In order to understand teenage drug use, it is imperative to recognize the context in which today's teens have grown up. Alcohol, tobacco, caffeine, over-the-counter and prescription drugs are everywhere. Though we urge our young people to be "drug-free," Americans are constantly bombarded with messages encouraging us to imbibe and medicate with a variety of substances. We use alcohol to celebrate ("Let's drink to that!"), to recreate ("I can't wait to kick back and have a cold one!") and even to medicate ("I really need a drink!"). We use caffeine to boost our energy, prescription and over-the-counter drugs to modify our moods, lift us out of depression and help us work, study and sleep.

Drugs are an integral part of American life. In fact, eight out of ten adults in the U.S. use at least one medication every week, and half take a prescription drug. One in two adults in this country use alcohol regularly; and more than 104 million Americans over the age of 12 have tried marijuana at some time in their lives—a fact not lost on their children.

Today's teenagers have witnessed first-hand the increasing, sometimes forced "Ritalinization" [Ritalin is a stimulant generally used to treat attention deficit disorder (ADD)] of their fellow students. Stimulants such as Adderal, an amphetamine product, have become a drug of choice on many college campuses. We see prime-time network commercials for drugs to manage such ailments as "Generalized Anxiety Disorder," and teenagers see increasing numbers of their parents using antidepressants to cope with life's problems.

While "peer pressure" is often blamed for teenage drug use, the 2008–2009 State of Our Nation's Youth survey found that, contrary to popular belief, most are not pressured to use drugs. Instead, teenage drug use seems to mirror modern American drug-taking tendencies. Some psychologists argue that given the nature of our culture, teenage experimentation with legal and illegal mind-altering substances should not be considered abnormal or deviant behavior. . . .

Honest, Science-Based Education

Surveys tell us that despite our admonitions and advice to abstain, large numbers of teenagers will occasionally experiment with intoxicating substances, and some will use alcohol and/or other drugs more regularly. This does not mean they are bad kids or we are neglectful parents. The reality is that drug use is a part of teenage culture in America today. In all likelihood, our young people will come out of this phase unharmed.

Keeping teenagers safe should be our highest priority. To protect them, a reality-based approach enables teenagers to make responsible decisions by:

- providing honest, science-based information;

- encouraging moderation if youthful experimentation persists;

- promoting an understanding of the legal and social consequences of drug use; and

- prioritizing safety through personal responsibility and knowledge.

Young people are capable of rational thinking. Although their decision-making skills will improve as they mature, teenagers are learning responsibility, and do not want to destroy their lives or their health.... According to the 2009 National Survey on Drug Use and Health, although experimentation is widespread, 90 percent of 12- to 17-year-olds choose to refrain from regular use.

Effective drug education should be based on sound science and acknowledge teenagers' ability to understand, analyze and evaluate. The subject of drugs can be integrated into a variety of high school courses and curricula, including physiology and biology (how drugs affect the body), psychology (how drugs affect the mind), chemistry (what's contained in drugs), social studies (who uses which drugs, and why) and history and civics (how drugs have been handled by various governments).

Rodney Skager, Professor Emeritus, University of California at Los Angeles and Chair of the California Statewide Task Force for Effective Drug Education, suggests that through family experience, peer exposure and the media, teenagers often know more about alcohol and other drugs than we assume. Therefore, students should be included in the development of drug education programs, and classes should utilize interaction and student participation rather than rote lecturing. If drug education is to be credible, formal curricula should incorporate the observations and experiences of young people themselves.

Teens clamor for honest, comprehensive drug education, and it is especially apparent when they leave home and go to college. According to Professor Craig Reinarman at the University of California at Santa Cruz:

> Students seem to hunger for information about licit and illicit drugs that doesn't strike them as moralistic propaganda. I've taught a large lecture course called "Drugs and Society" for over twenty years and each year I have to turn away dozens of students because the class fills up so quickly.
>
> I always start by asking them, "How many of you had drug education in high school?" and nearly all of them raise their hands. Then I ask, "How many of you felt it was truthful and valuable?" Out of 120 students, perhaps three hands go up.

The Importance of Moderation

The vast majority of teenage drug use (with the exception of nicotine) does not lead to dependence or abusive habits.

Teens who do use alcohol, marijuana and/or other drugs must understand there is a huge difference between use and abuse, and between occasional and daily use.

They should know how to recognize irresponsible behavior when it comes to place, time, dose levels and frequency of use. If young people continue, despite our admonitions, to use alcohol and/or other drugs, they must control their use by practicing moderation and limiting use. It is impossible to do well academically or meet one's responsibilities at work while intoxicated. It is never appropriate to use alcohol and/or other drugs at school, at work, while participating in sports, while driving or engaging in any serious activity.

Understanding Consequences

Young people must understand the consequences of violating school rules and local and state laws against the use, possession and sale of alcohol and other drugs—whether or not they agree with such policies.

With increasing methods of detection such as school-based drug testing and zero-tolerance policies, illegality is a risk in and of itself which extends beyond the physical effects of drug use. There are real, lasting consequences of using drugs and being caught, including expulsion from school, a criminal record and social stigma. The Higher Education Act—now being challenged by many organizations, including Students for Sensible Drug Policy (www.ssdp.org)—has resulted in the denial of college loans for more than 200,000 U.S. students convicted of any drug offense. This law was scaled back in 2006, but the penalty still applies to students who are convicted while they are enrolled in school. . . .

The Role of Parents

Today's parents get more advice, too often in excruciating detail, about how to raise their children, than any generation in history. Yet they're open and listening because they're concerned about their teens' safety and well-being, and worried that the world has become a much more dangerous place. They want to know what to do, and are looking for solutions.

There are no easy answers, but for parents who have requested specifics, here are the steps I suggest:

Step 1: Listen. The first step is to "get real" about drug use by listening to what teens have to tell us about their lives and their feelings. This will guide us toward intelligent, thoughtful action.

A useful venue is the dinner table. As much as possible, families should eat together once a day so they can "catch up," talk and otherwise connect.

Why Do Young People Use Drugs?

Prevention experts have identified "risk factors" and "protective factors" to help determine how drug abuse begins and how it progresses. Risk factors can increase a person's chances for drug abuse, and protective factors can reduce the risks. It's important to remember that not everyone at risk for drug abuse actually becomes a drug user.

Here are some early signs of risk that may predict later drug use:

- Association with drug abusing peers
- A lack of attachment and nurturing by parents or caregivers
- Ineffective parenting
- A caregiver who abuses drugs
- Aggressive behavior
- Lack of self-control
- Poor classroom behavior or social skills
- Academic failure

Young people are most vulnerable to drug use during times of transition; for instance, when teens make the switch from elementary to middle school or when they enter high school, new social and emotional challenges affect them on many levels.

US Department of Justice,
Drug Prevention 4 Teens,
2008. www.justice.gov.

There are many other natural openings for conversation, such as drug use in movies, television and music. If we can remain as non-judgmental as possible, teenagers will seek our opinions and guidance. Let them know they can talk freely. Our greatest challenge is to listen and try to help without excessive admonishment. If we become indignant and punitive, teenagers will stop talking to us. It's that simple.

Remember that advice is most likely to be heard when it is requested. Realize that teens bring their own experiences to the table, some of which you may not want to hear. But breathe deeply and be grateful when they share these experiences because this means you have established trust.

Step 2: Learn. Parents and teachers need to take responsibility for learning about the physiological, psychological and sociological effects of alcohol and other drugs. This involves reading and asking questions.

Familiarize yourself with teenage culture through print and electronic media, especially the Internet. Watch MTV [Music Television, a cable channel]. Learn about the array of drugs available to young people, but be sure your sources are scientifically grounded and balanced. Any source that fails to describe both risks and benefits should be considered suspect. . . .

Step 3: Act. Drug abuse prevention is not a curriculum package or a "magic bullet," so make some plans.

It is important to keep teens engaged and busy, not just during the school day, but from 3 to 6 P.M., when the use of drugs by bored, unsupervised teens is highest. Extracurricular programs such as sports, arts, drama and other creative activities should be available to all secondary school students, at low or no cost to parents. Become an advocate for such programs in your community and teens' school.

Prevention is fundamentally about caring, connected relationships and an open exchange of information. There are no easy answers, just thoughtful conversations. . . .

Many parents today have experimented with drugs. The question, "What should I tell my child about my own past drug use?" comes up [often]. Many parents are uneasy about revealing their own experience, fearing such admissions might open the door to their own teen's experimentation.

There is no one simple resolution to this difficult dilemma. While you do not need to rehash every detail, it can be very helpful to share your own experiences with your teen because it makes you a more credible confidant.

Honesty is usually the best policy in the long run. Just as parents often know or eventually find out when their child is lying, teenagers have a knack for seeing through adults' evasions, half-truths and hypocrisy. Besides, if you don't tell, you can rest assured that eventually one of your siblings or close friends will delight in recounting your "youthful indiscretions" to your eager child.

Trusting relationships are key in preventing and countering drug use. While it is tempting to cut through difficult conversations and utilize detection technologies such as urine testing, think hard before you demand that your child submit to a drug test. Random, suspicionless school-based drug testing—which has been opposed by the California State Parent Teacher Association (PTA)—has been shown to be ineffective and often counterproductive.

Regarding in-home test kits, researchers at Children's Hospital in Boston, who studied home drug testing products, warn that most people are not appropriately educated about the limitations and technical challenges of drug tests (including collection procedures, the potential for misinterpretation and false positive/negative results). They also note unanticipated consequences and the negative effect on parent-child relationships of collecting a urine sample to ascertain drug use.

The reality is that a trusting, open relationship with a parent or other respected adult can be the most powerful element in deterring abusive patterns. And trust, once lost, can be hard to regain.

Perhaps most important, teenagers need to know that the important adults in their lives are concerned primarily with their safety; that they have someone to turn to when they need help. If they find themselves in a compromising or uncomfortable situation, they need to know we will come to their aid immediately.

> "We should prepare young adults to make responsible decisions about alcohol in the same way we prepare them to operate a motor vehicle."

Drinking Age of 21 Doesn't Work

John M. McCardell Jr.

In the following viewpoint, John M. McCardell Jr. contends that laws making it illegal to purchase and drink alcohol while under the age of twenty-one has not prevented underage drinking; in fact, binge drinking among young adults is on the rise. Mc-Cardell suggests that young people should be educated about responsible drinking habits and then issued a license that allows them to purchase and consume alcohol so long as they demonstrate their ability to follow the law. John M. McCardell Jr. is the founder and president of Choose Responsibility, a nonprofit organization that seeks to engage the public in debate over the effects of the twenty-one-year-old drinking age.

As you read, consider the following questions:

1. What did the 1984 National Minimum Drinking Age Act threaten to withhold from states that did not abide by the legal drinking age of twenty-one, according to McCardell?

2. According to McCardell, have alcohol-related fatalities risen or declined since 1984?

3. Do most other countries enforce a legal drinking age of twenty-one, according to McCardell?

One year ago [2008], a group of college and university presidents and chancellors, eventually totaling 135, issued a statement that garnered national attention.

The "Amethyst Initiative" put a debate proposition before the public—"Resolved: That the 21-year-old drinking age is not working." It offered, in much the way a grand jury performs its duties, sufficient evidence for putting the proposition to the test. It invited informed and dispassionate public debate and committed the signatory institutions to encouraging that debate. And it called on elected officials not to continue assuming that, after 25 years, the status quo could not be challenged, even improved.

Binge Drinking on the Rise

One year later, the drinking age debate continues, and new research reinforces the presidential impulse. Just this summer [2009] a study published in the *Journal of the American Academy of Child and Adolescent Psychiatry* revealed that, among college-age males, binge drinking is unchanged from its levels of 1979; that among non-college women it has increased by 20 percent; and that among college women it has increased by 40 percent.

Remarkably, the counterintuitive conclusion drawn by the investigators, and accepted uncritically by the media, including editorials in *The New York Times* and *The Washington Post* is that the study proves that raising the drinking age to 21 has been a success.

More recently, a study of binge drinking published in the *Journal of the American Medical Association* announced that "despite efforts at prevention, the prevalence of binge drinking among college students is continuing to rise, and so are the harms associated with it."

Worse still, a related study has shown that habits formed at 18 die hard: "For each year studied, a greater percentage of 21- to 24-year-olds [those who were of course once 18, 19 and 20] engaged in binge drinking and driving under the influence of alcohol."

Influenced by the Threat of Withheld Funds

Yet, in the face of mounting evidence that those young adults age 18 to 20 toward whom the drinking age law has been directed are routinely—indeed in life- and health-threatening ways—violating it, there remains a belief in the land that a minimum drinking age of 21 has been a "success." And elected officials are periodically reminded of a provision in the 1984 law that continues to stifle any serious public debate in our country's state legislative chambers: Any state that sets its drinking age lower than 21 forfeits 10 percent of its annual federal highway appropriation.

But it's not 1984 anymore.

This statement may seem obvious, but not necessarily. In 1984 Congress passed and the president signed the National Minimum Drinking Age Act. The Act, which raised the drinking age to 21 under threat of highway fund withholding, sought to address the problem of drunken driving fatalities. And indeed, that problem was serious.

States that lowered their ages during the 1970s and did nothing else to prepare young adults to make responsible decisions about alcohol witnessed an alarming increase in alcohol-related traffic fatalities. It was as though the driving age were lowered but no drivers' education were provided. The results were predictable.

Now, 25 years later, we are in a much different, and better, place. Thanks to the effective public advocacy of organizations like Mothers Against Drunk Driving, we are far more aware of the risks of drinking and driving. Automobiles are much safer.

Seatbelts and airbags are mandatory. The "designated driver" is now a part of our vocabulary. And more and more states are mandating ignition interlocks for first-time DUI offenders, perhaps the most effective way to get drunken drivers off the road.

And the statistics are encouraging. Alcohol-related fatalities have declined over the last 25 years [since 1984]. Better still, they have declined in all age groups, though the greatest number of deaths occurs at age 21, followed by 22 and 23. We are well on the way to solving a problem that vexed us 25 years ago.

A Different Problem Today than in 1984

The problem today [2009] is different. The problem today is reckless, goal-oriented alcohol consumption that all too often takes place in clandestine locations, where enforcement has proven frustratingly difficult. Alcohol consumption among young adults is not taking place in public places or public view or in the presence of other adults who might help model responsible behavior. But we know it is taking place.

If not in public, then where? The college presidents who signed the Amethyst Initiative know where. It happens in "pre-gaming" sessions in locked dorm rooms where students take multiple shots of hard alcohol in rapid succession, before going to a social event where alcohol is not served. It happens in off-campus apartments beyond college boundaries and thus

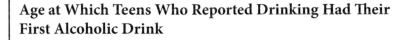

Age at Which Teens Who Reported Drinking Had Their First Alcoholic Drink

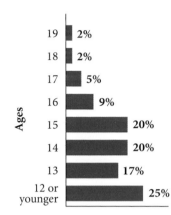

Ages

19	2%
18	2%
17	5%
16	9%
15	20%
14	20%
13	17%
12 or younger	25%

Average age when teens had first drink = 14.
62% of teens had had their first drink by age 15.

TAKEN FROM: The Partnership at DrugFree.org, "Study on Teen Substance Abuse Highlights Need for Screening and Prevention Programs," April 19, 2001. www.drugfree.org.

beyond the presidents' authority; and it happens in remote fields to which young adults must drive.

And the Amethyst presidents know the deadly result: Of the 5,000 lives lost to alcohol each year by those under 21, more than 60 percent are lost OFF the roadways, according to the National Institute of Alcoholism and Alcohol Abuse.

The principal problem of 2009 is not drunken driving. The principal problem of 2009 is clandestine binge drinking.

That is why the Amethyst presidents believe a public debate is so urgent. The law does not say drink responsibly or drink in moderation. It says don't drink. To those affected by it, those who in the eyes of the law are, in every other respect legal adults, it is Prohibition. And it is incomprehensible.

The principal impediment to public debate is the 10 percent highway penalty. That penalty should be waived for those states that choose to try something different, which may turn out to be something better. But merely adjusting the age—up or down—is not really the way to make a change.

Educating and Licensing for Responsible Drinking

We should prepare young adults to make responsible decisions about alcohol in the same way we prepare them to operate a motor vehicle: by first educating and then licensing, and permitting them to exercise the full privileges of adulthood so long as they demonstrate their ability to observe the law.

Licensing would work like drivers education—it would involve a permit, perhaps graduated, allowing the holder the privilege of purchasing, possessing and consuming alcohol, as each state determined, so long as the holder had passed an alcohol education course and observed the alcohol laws of the issuing state.

Most of the rest of the world has come out in a different place on the drinking age. The United States is one of only four countries—the others are Indonesia, Mongolia and Palau—with an age as high as 21. All others either have no minimum age or have a lower age, generally 18, with some at 16.

Young adults know that. And, in their heart of hearts, they also know that a law perceived as unjust, a law routinely violated, can over time breed disrespect for law in general.

Slowly but surely we may be seeing a change in attitude. This summer [2009], Dr. Morris Chafetz, a distinguished psychiatrist, a member of the presidential commission that recommended raising the drinking age, and the founder of the National Institute for Alcoholism and Alcohol Abuse admitted that supporting the higher drinking age is "the most regrettable decision of my entire professional career." This remarkable statement did not receive the attention it merited.

Alcohol is a reality in the lives of young adults. We can either try to change the reality—which has been our principal focus since 1984, by imposing Prohibition on young adults 18 to 20—or we can create the safest possible environment for the reality.

A drinking age minimum of 21 has not changed the reality. It's time to try something different.

It's not 1984 anymore.

"Lowering the drinking age ... will increase heavy drinking and the problems that accompany it in college communities and push the problem back into high schools."

Lowering the Legal Drinking Age Will Not Encourage Responsible Drinking Habits

Toben F. Nelson, Traci L. Toomey, John R. Finnegan Jr., Henry Wechsler, Robert Saltz, James Fell, Thomas Greenfield, Ann Mahoney, and Linda Bosma

In the following viewpoint, Toben Nelson, Traci Toomey and their coauthors contend that lowering the legal drinking age will not lead to less alcohol-related problems among students, but in fact would actually increase drunk-driving accidents and emergency room visits. The authors further maintain that in countries with lower age limits, the rates of binge drinking and resulting problems are higher than in the United States. Toben F. Nelson and Traci L. Toomey are members of the faculty of the University of Minnesota's School of Public Health and of the staff of the Alcohol Epidemiology Program. John R. Finnegan Jr.

is dean of the University of Minnesota School of Public Health, Henry Wechsler is director of the Harvard School of Public Health College Alcohol Study, Robert Saltz and James Fell are with the Pacific Institute for Research and Evaluation, Thomas Greenfield is with the Alcohol Research Group at the Public Health Institute, and Ann Mahoney and Linda Bosma are the current Chair and Chair-elect of the Alcohol, Tobacco and Other Drugs section of the American Public Health Association.

As you read, consider the following questions:

1. According to the authors, in what decade did many US states reduce their legal drinking age, and what was the result?

2. Do underage college students binge drink more or less than students over twenty-one years of age, according to the authors?

3. Do college presidents believe the legal drinking age of twenty-one has effectively solved most alcohol-related problems on their campuses, according to the authors?

The national policy that set a minimum legal drinking age of 21 is being questioned by a group of 135 college and university presidents through an effort called the Amethyst Initiative.

In a September 16 [2009] commentary on CNN.com, Amethyst Initiative leader John McCardell, a former president of Middlebury College, proposes lowering the drinking age, which he suggests will lead to less drinking and related problems among college students.

History and a comprehensive review of the research tell a much different story. The evidence is clear, consistent and compelling: A drinking age of 21 has led to less drinking, fewer injuries and fewer deaths.

Lowering the Drinking Age Was Tried and Failed

In the 1970s when many states reduced their drinking ages, drinking-related deaths among young people increased. When the drinking age of 21 was restored, deaths declined. This effect is not simply a historical artifact explained by advances in safety technology and other policies.

New Zealand recently lowered the drinking age based on many of the same arguments advanced by the Amethyst Initiative. The result was more alcohol-involved traffic crashes and emergency room visits among 15- to 19-year-olds. New Zealand is now considering raising its drinking age. The National Highway Traffic Safety Administration estimates that setting the drinking age at 21 saves the lives of 900 young people each year and has saved more than 25,000 lives since 1975.

It was on the basis of compelling research evidence about its lifesaving benefits that a bipartisan effort created Public Law 98-363, "The National Minimum Legal Drinking Age Act" in the first place. Subsequent research has strengthened the evidence. College students who are underage, for example, binge drink less than students aged 21–23.

Enforcing the Legal Drinking Age Reduces Binge Drinking

Underage students who attend colleges that rigorously enforce the drinking age, and who reside in states that have more laws restricting access to alcohol for those under the legal age, are less likely to binge drink.

Another myth promulgated by the Amethyst Initiative is that European young people are taught by families to drink responsibly because of the typically lower legal drinking ages there. The reverse is the case. Surveys of youth in multiple European countries show that rates of frequent binge drinking among adolescents are higher in Europe than in the United States.

Panels of experts, convened separately by the National Institute on Alcohol Abuse and Alcoholism, the Substance Abuse and Mental Health Services Administration, the National Academy of Sciences Institute of Medicine and the Centers for Disease Control and Prevention have studied the evidence on the age-21 law and concluded that it is effective public policy. Rather than lowering the drinking age, they recommended bolstering the law by closing loopholes in state law and strengthening enforcement.

There is a silver lining to the call for reopening discussion on the minimum legal drinking age. While some college presidents have signed on to the Amethyst Initiative, most have not.

College presidents acknowledge that a serious problem exists on their campuses and that something needs to be done. Working effectively with their communities and states to address student drinking is the place to start, not with a discussion about lowering the drinking age.

College presidents must show leadership by promoting solutions recommended by a report from the National Institute on Alcohol Abuse and Alcoholism College Drinking Task Force released in 2002.

The Solution Is Tougher Restrictions— Not Leniency

These recommendations for college and community leaders included creating systems for reaching individual students with effective interventions, implementing, publicizing and enforcing laws to prevent alcohol-impaired driving and underage drinking, restrictions on alcohol retail outlets, increasing prices and excise taxes on alcoholic beverages, and responsible

'Well I don't care if your combined age is around 50...I'm not selling you alcohol.'

beverage service policies at on- and off-campus venues. Few colleges and their communities have even begun the steps needed to enact these efforts.

These recommendations will be difficult to implement and significant barriers exist, including resistance from the industries that profit from selling alcohol. College presidents cannot accomplish this alone. They need the support of students, regents, parents, alumni and their communities.

State and local legislators need to pass tougher restrictions and provide resources for enforcement. Lobbying legislators to dismantle the effective drinking age law is a step in the wrong direction.

So rather than try the approaches advocated by the Amethyst Initiative that have no foundation in research, let's be clear about the issues.

College student drinking is a serious problem. Each year more young people are injured, sexually assaulted and die as the result of drinking. These statistics would be even worse without the age-21 law.

Lowering the drinking age will not save lives or make our campuses and communities better places to live. It will increase heavy drinking and the problems that accompany it in college communities and push the problem back into high schools. Real prevention requires constant vigilance, dedication and the courage to implement difficult solutions.

| "If every state increased its cigarette tax rate by \$1.00 per pack, 1.7 million kids will be prevented from becoming addicted adult smokers . . . and more than 900,000 lives will be saved."

Marketing Restrictions and Tobacco Tax Increases Will Reduce Tobacco Addiction

Campaign for Tobacco-Free Kids, Counter Tobacco, and the American Heart Association

In the following viewpoint, Campaign for Tobacco-Free Kids, Counter Tobacco, and the American Heart Association maintain that increasing the tobacco tax will prevent kids from starting to smoke and will encourage active smokers to quit. These organizations also suggest that restrictions on selling tobacco products near youth-frequented areas, prohibitions on tobacco product discounts, and requirements that tobacco packages be stored out of view will help prevent tobacco addiction. The Campaign for Tobacco-Free Kids advocates for public policies that reduce tobacco use and exposure to secondhand smoke. Counter Tobacco is an organization that works to counteract tobacco product sales and marketing at the point of sale. The American Heart Association is the oldest and largest voluntary organization devoted to fighting cardiovascular disease and stroke in the United States.

As you read, consider the following questions:

1. According to Campaign for Tobacco-Free Kids, Counter Tobacco, and the American Heart Association, how many kids try their first cigarette every day?

2. Is the majority of the voting public against an increase in tobacco taxes, according to these organizations?

3. Are "light" and "low-tar" cigarettes less harmful than regular cigarettes, according to these organizations?

In reality, increasing the tobacco tax is a win-win-win for states. It is a win for public health because it will reduce tobacco use and its devastating health effects. It is a win for state budgets because, despite declines in tobacco consumption, it will produce significant new revenue and reduce health care costs. Finally, as state and national polls show, it is a political win for policy makers, as large majorities of voters across the political spectrum and around the country support tobacco tax increases. The new revenue can also be used to fund tobacco prevention and cessation programs. Tobacco tax increases could also be a win for retailers, who could break their unhealthy alliance with tobacco companies while earning profits from other goods.

WIN #1: A Health Win

Tobacco tax increases prevent kids from starting to smoke, encourage smokers to quit and save lives and health care dollars. Each year, 443,000 Americans die from tobacco use—the leading preventable cause of death in the country. Every day, nearly 4,000 kids try their first cigarette, and another 1,000 kids become regular smokers.

Studies have shown that for every 10 percent increase in the price of cigarettes, youth smoking declines by approximately seven percent, smoking among pregnant women falls at a similar rate, and overall consumption declines by about four percent. . . .

As prices climbed in the late 1990s and early 2000s, youth smoking rates declined. But as the price leveled off and even decreased between 2003 and 2005 (along with reduced funding for tobacco prevention programs in many states), progress in reducing youth smoking stalled, and youth smoking rates even increased in 2005.

The Campaign for Tobacco-Free Kids estimates that if every state increased its cigarette tax rate by 50 cents per pack to counteract the 50-cents per pack discount from the cigarette companies' price promotions, more than 850,000 kids will be prevented from becoming addicted adult smokers, more than 700,000 adults will quit, and more than 460,000 lives will be saved. If every state increased its cigarette tax rate by $1.00 per pack, 1.7 million kids will be prevented from becoming addicted adult smokers, 1.4 million adults will quit, and more than 900,000 lives will be saved.

WIN #2: A Budget Win

Despite what the tobacco industry and its allies claim, every single state that has raised its cigarette tax rate significantly has generated dramatic new revenue despite the declines in smoking that occur as a result of the price increase. This is simply because the increased tax per pack brings in more new state revenue than is lost from the related reductions in the number of packs sold and taxed in the state.

The higher revenue levels enjoyed by those states that significantly increase their cigarette tax rates persist over time, while the health care savings from the related declines in smoking grow rapidly. . . .

States will realize even more revenue if they also increase the tax on other tobacco products (OTPs), to deter children from experimenting with these products and encourage smokers to quit rather than switch to a lower-cost option.

Tobacco tax increases will produce other economic benefits. State budgets will gain from the declines in smoking and consequent drop in smoking-caused health care costs. Each year in the U.S., smoking-caused disease results in $96 billion in health care costs, much of which is paid by taxpayers through higher insurance premiums and government-funded health programs such as Medicaid. Indeed, higher Medicaid costs are one of the reasons states are facing budget difficulties. By reducing smoking, tobacco tax increases will reduce smoking-related health care costs.

The Campaign for Tobacco-Free Kids estimates that nationally, if each state increased its tobacco tax by $1.00 per pack, it would reduce immediate health care costs by billions of dollars and long-term health care costs by more than $58 billion. In the first five years, health care costs would decline just from fewer smoking-caused heart attacks and strokes and fewer smoking-affected births. Overall health care savings would grow over the lifetimes of the smokers who quit or kids who never start smoking because of the $1.00 increase.

WIN #3: A Political Win

State and national polls show that large majorities of voters of both major parties and virtually all demographic groups support increasing tobacco taxes and candidates who vote to support them. Not only do voters support significant tobacco tax increases, they far prefer tobacco tax increases to other options for balancing budgets, such as other tax increases or cutting programs such as health, education and transportation.

Tobacco companies and their allies will say and do anything to oppose tobacco tax increases, including creating front groups and recruiting retailers to parrot the industry's false

Tobacco Use in Movie Trailers

Depictions of smoking in movie trailers [commercials for movies] have important implications for exposure as the trailers are aired on television and may be seen by a wider audience than the movie itself. One study combined a content analysis of trailers with Nielsen [an information and measurement company that provides market research] data measuring media exposure among 12- to 17-year-olds; of all 216 movie trailers shown on television in a single year (2001–2002), 14.4% included images of tobacco use. Nielsen data indicated that during that year 95% of all U.S. youth aged 12–17 years saw at least one movie trailer on television depicting the use of tobacco, and 88.8% saw at least one of these trailers three or more times. Over the course of that year, movie trailers showing tobacco use were seen 270 million times by youth aged 12–17 years. One experimental study found that smoking by a character in a film trailer was associated with increased perceptions of that character's attractiveness among adolescent smokers.

US Department of Health and Human Services,
*Preventing Tobacco Use Among Youth and Young Adults:
A Report of the Surgeon General.* Rockville, MD:
US Department of Health and Human Services, 2012.

claims. However, that doesn't change the fact that the tobacco industry and retailers know that tobacco tax increases will reduce tobacco use.

Restrictions on Point-of-Sale Marketing

Reducing the impact of point-of-sale marketing is part of a comprehensive strategy to prevent kids from using tobacco and reduce overall tobacco use. The 2009 Tobacco Control Act included significant restrictions on how tobacco products are sold and marketed in stores. The law established a nationwide prohibition on tobacco sales to children under 18, required photo ID checks for sales to anyone appearing under 27 years of age and provided for tough federal enforcement and penalties against retailers who sell to minors. The law also prohibited:

- The sale of candy and fruit-flavored cigarettes

- Self-service displays of cigarettes and smokeless tobacco (except in adult-only facilities)

- Non-tobacco gifts with purchase, such as T-shirts, hats and lighters

- Use of misleading terms such as "light" and "low-tar" that falsely imply some cigarettes are less harmful.

The law also requires large, graphic health warnings on cigarettes and restricted tobacco ads to black-and-white text only at the point of sale, outdoors and in magazines with significant youth readership. But these provisions are on hold pending resolution of lawsuits filed by tobacco companies. The law also directed [the] FDA [Food and Drug Administration] to develop regulations that would restrict tobacco advertising near schools and playgrounds.

In addition to these specific provisions, the law granted the FDA the authority to further restrict tobacco marketing to the extent allowed by the First Amendment to the Constitution. It also gave state and local governments new authority to regulate the time, place, and manner (but not content) of tobacco advertising, consistent with the First Amendment, and preserved the authority of states and localities to adopt other measures to reduce tobacco use.

At the state and local level, in addition to increasing tobacco taxes, implementing comprehensive smoke-free laws, and ensuring sufficient funding for tobacco prevention programs, point-of-sale regulation has become an emerging core strategy to reduce tobacco use. . . .

Restrictions on Licensing and Zoning Policies

Licensing and zoning policies impact how and where tobacco products are sold through the number, type, location, and density of tobacco retailers. They provide local and state governments effective opportunities to protect their citizens from the harmful effects of tobacco and limit youth exposure to tobacco.

Licensing and zoning rules can limit retailer locations and put restrictions on product sales methods and placement. These policies can require all retailers to register their businesses and set zoning restrictions to prevent future tobacco retailers from setting up shop near schools, playgrounds or other youth-frequented places. The requirements for obtaining and maintaining licenses can also include provisions that specifies where, how and what types of tobacco products are sold and can even prohibit the redemption of coupons. . . .

Point-of-Sale Health Warnings

Point-of-sale health warnings are meant to ensure that both smokers and non-smokers are well aware of the many specific health effects of cigarettes and other tobacco products. This counter-advertising mechanism involves placing written and pictorial warnings of the health impacts of tobacco usage in a retail environment, together with information about cessation services. . . .

Raising Tobacco Prices Through Nontax Approaches

Raising the price of tobacco products is the most potent strategy for reducing overall tobacco consumption. When prices go up, fewer kids start using tobacco and more adults try to quit or reduce consumption. Raising tobacco prices is also a public policy that can garner broad public support, especially when monies raised are funneled back into tobacco control or other health programs.

Increasing cigarette excise taxes is the most direct way to raise prices and reduce consumption. However, there are additional strategies to increase the price of tobacco products. It is important to use multiple methods to keep prices high because tobacco companies can easily undermine a single pricing policy with discounting.

Non-tax approaches to raising cigarette prices include:

1. *Strong tobacco product minimum price laws* set a floor price for tobacco products, prohibiting tobacco products from being sold for less than this price. Setting a floor price can counteract industry-supported discounts. As of December 31, 2009, 25 states (including Washington, DC) had minimum price laws, with a median markup at the wholesale level of 4 percent and a median markup at the retail level of 8 percent.

2. *Prohibiting price discounting/multipack offers* prevents tobacco companies from discounting prices at select stores, select areas, or at select times (e.g., around the time of a tax hike). This eliminates the industry's ability to target discounts to reach consumers when they are particularly price-conscious.

3. *Increasing retailer licensing fees* will likely force retailers to pass on their additional costs to the consumer, thereby raising cigarette prices. These fees should be used to improve enforcement and monitoring of these stores.

4. *Mitigation fees,* such as cigarette butt litter mitigation fees, increase the overall cost of tobacco products and are used for a specific purpose, not for general revenue.

By themselves, these fees may not be large enough to significantly impact tobacco use, but they can help offset industry strategies to reduce price in addition to the primary benefit of reducing litter.

5. *Disclosure or sunshine laws* to require tobacco companies to disclose the amount of money they provide for price discounting to retailers for a specific geographic area, such as a city or a state.

Product placement restrictions—full or partial—require storing tobacco packages out of view of the customer, often under the counter, in closed drawers or covered cabinets. While no government in the U.S. has yet implemented this policy, other countries including Australia, Iceland, Thailand and much of Canada have prohibited tobacco product displays in the retail environment.

The Partnership Between Convenience Stores and Big Tobacco

As this report demonstrates, the point-of-sale has become the dominant channel for the marketing of deadly and addictive tobacco products in the United States. Such marketing provides the tobacco industry with a highly effective way of enticing kids to start using tobacco, encourage continued tobacco use and discourage quitting among current users, target minority communities and portray tobacco products as appealing and acceptable.

In addition, convenience stores have become essential partners with the tobacco industry in fighting tobacco tax increases and other policies to reduce tobacco use.

This powerful alliance between Big Tobacco [a nickname for the tobacco industry] and convenience stores poses a serious threat to efforts to reduce tobacco use, the leading cause of preventable death in the United States. It is critical that elected officials reject the influence of these special interests and take action to protect our nation's children and health instead. They should do so by adopting policies that include tobacco tax increases, restrictions on tobacco marketing and the other point-of-sale tobacco control policies described in this report. Such actions are critical to continued progress and eventually winning the fight against tobacco use.

Periodical and Internet Sources Bibliography

The following articles have been selected to supplement the diverse views presented in this chapter.

Greg Bolt	"Smoking Ban Debate Reignites," *Register-Guard*, September 30, 2012.
Janice D'Arcy	"Teen Pot Use Is Up. Could Parents Be to Blame?" *Washington Post*, December 15, 2011.
Elizabeth Donovan	"Why Teens, Parents, and Alcohol Don't Mix," *Psychology Today*, May 10, 2011.
Jennifer Matesa	"Is Your Kid an Addict?" *Salon*, September 27, 2012.
Gabriel Mateus	"Prevent Teens' Easy Alcohol Access," *U-T San Diego*, July 6, 2013.
National Institute on Drug Abuse	"Frequently Asked Questions About Drug Testing in Schools," National Institute on Drug Abuse, November 2011.
Mary Pilon	"Middle Schools Add a Team Rule: Get a Drug Test," *New York Times*, September 22, 2012.
Tina Rosenberg	"For Teenage Smokers, Removing the Allure of the Pack," *New York Times*, August 1, 2012.
Mike Steinberger	"Should You Let Your Kids Try Wine?" *Slate*, March 21, 2012.
Gary Strauss	"Graphic Cigarette Labels, Will They Work?" *USA Today*, August 22, 2011.
Will Wooton	"Is There Value to Drug Testing?" *Pomerado News*, September 13, 2012.

How Do Addictions Affect Relationships?

Chapter Preface

Enable: to provide with the means or opportunity; to make possible, practical, or easy. Viewed a certain way, enabling is a constructive and beneficial behavior. Parents work hard and make sacrifices to provide a safe and supportive home environment, *enabling* their children to thrive. People offer encouragement and assistance in caring for loved ones who are sick, *enabling* them to become well. Philanthropists contribute their time or money to the poor and needy, *enabling* them to eat nutritious food and drink clean water. Viewed another way, however, *enabling* is a misguided behavior. For example, wives who make excuses to others for their alcoholic husbands when they are absent from work, social events, or their children's activities are *enabling* their husbands to continue their substance abuse. In fact, when used in connection with addiction or any other unacceptable behavior, the word "enable" is a very bad word indeed.

Shades of Hope, a treatment center in Texas, defines *enabling* as "an adaptive behavior adopted by people who live with addicts. Whenever you allow an addict to continue their addictive behavior, whether actively or passively, you are enabling." And according to Peggy L. Ferguson, author of the book *Family Dynamics of Addiction and Recovery*, a good definition of *enabling* is simply "removing the natural negative consequences of someone's behavior." Many experts believe addiction changes a person's thinking processes and causes one to disregard his or her customary sense of right and wrong. Once addicted, most addicts will do anything, including lie, cheat, and steal, to get that next drink, hit, or fix. Thus, family members and loved ones of addicts find themselves in the difficult position of watching the addict and the relationship deteriorate while at the same time trying to continue their lives as usual, hoping that their love and support will draw the addict back to sobriety. They want to empower their loved one to get back on his or her feet, but their misguided efforts often just enable the addict instead. In their book *The Anatomy of Addiction: Overcoming the Triggers That Stand in the Way of Recovery*, husband and wife psychoanalysts Morteza Khaleghi and Karen Khaleghi explain the difference between empowering and enabling this way: "Empowering someone is doing something for someone or helping him to do something that he does not have the capacity to do himself; enabling is doing something for someone that she can do, or very well ought to be doing, for herself." They also write, "Shielding someone from the consequences of his or her actions is, to put it plainly, a way of causing harm. . . . Enabling is a major factor in the perpetuation of addiction."

Addiction changes the dynamics in relationships, and fear for loved ones and uncertainty about the future loom large. But most addiction experts agree that actions must have consequences, and the most successful path to recovery—for the addict and for his or her relationships with others—is through accountability, not through enabling.

> "Family therapy sessions offer an excellent opportunity to address the family dynamics, discuss past hurts and rebuild damaged relationships."

Addiction Recovery Can Strengthen Relationships

Alan Goodstat

In the following viewpoint, Alan Goodstat explains that most addiction recovery programs involve therapy in which the entire family takes part. He maintains that if family members participate with open and honest communication, damaged relationships can be rebuilt with stronger and healthier bonds. Alan Goodstat, who holds a master's degree in social work from Columbia University, is senior vice president and chief compliant officer at a private drug and alcohol rehabilitation center in Florida.

As you read, consider the following questions:

1. According to Alan Goodstat, what is one way addiction recovery can help children of addicts?

2. According to Goodstat, forgiveness, one of the most common principles of recovery, must manifest in what form?

3. Is becoming a mentor to other recovering addicts advised, according to Goodstat?

Addiction in a marriage is never a good thing. The drug or alcohol becomes almost like a third person in the relationship and drives a wedge between spouses. The personality of the addict and spouse changes, which alters the dynamic of the marriage. However, odd as it may seem, there are ways that recovery from addiction can end up saving your marriage. Here's how:

Therapy for the Whole Family

Addiction recovery will involve therapy of some kind. For addicts who are married or have a family, it often involves therapy sessions in which the entire family participates. These family therapy sessions offer an excellent opportunity to address the family dynamics, discuss past hurts and rebuild damaged relationships. Doing so will cause you to come out with a stronger marriage, a renewed sense of trust in each other, and a deeper bond.

Without therapy, the marriage and family relationships may languish in the same dysfunctional interactions that arose as a result of the addiction. The behavior of the addict during the addiction likely caused significant damage to family relationships. Trust was replaced with deceit. Integrity was replaced with lies. If these emotions and actions are allowed to remain, the likelihood of the marriage surviving is very small.

Children Benefit from Family Therapy

Therapy can help families work through the emotional and mental component of addiction and its impact on the entire family. Through therapy, the addict and spouse or family members can regain open and honest communication, rebuild trust, foster forgiveness and learn self-acceptance. Once the old wounds have been brought out into the open, family recovery can begin to take place.

Family therapy provides a necessary and safe environment for children of addicts as well. Not only can children of addicts play a part in their parents' recovery, family therapy can also serve as an intervention for at-risk children of addicts. These children may be on the path to addiction themselves, as a result of having to grow up with addiction in the family as well as genetic factors. Early intervention can help prevent children from following in their parents' footsteps.

Principles of Recovery Can Also Help Marriage

The principles learned during recovery from addiction can also assist in improving the marriage. A principle is a basic action or guideline that the addict has committed to following as he or she progresses through recovery from addiction. Principles become a way of life for recovering addicts and their families.

The principles of recovery from addiction will vary from person to person, but the most common core principles are taken from the 12 steps to recovery:

- *Honesty*—The addict openly and honestly faces up to their addiction and commits him or herself to honest interactions henceforth.

- *Hope*—As it pertains to the hope the addict can develop as recovery progresses. Hope of recovery is a powerful motivator.

- *Faith*—This can refer to having faith in yourself, your spouse or in a higher power, any of which can pull you through the tough times.

- *Courage*—This refers to the courage to openly and honestly confront yourself, your addictions and related actions.

- *Integrity*—The ability to own up to our past mistakes and take responsibility for them.

- *Willingness*—Willingness to change and willingness to let go of destructive habits.

- *Humility*—A willingness to ask for help when needed.

- *Discipline and Action*—Committed actions to support recovery from addiction and repair relationships.

- *Forgiveness*—Asking for forgiveness from those you have hurt through your addictions. The forgiveness must come in the form of actions, not just words.

- *Acceptance*—Admitting mistakes and accepting others and yourself.

- *Knowledge and Awareness*—Becoming aware of yourself as you move through life and having awareness of your life's purpose. This principle requires you to try to do the right thing in all actions.

- *Service and Gratitude*—Serving as a mentor to other recovering addicts and expressing gratitude for the accomplishments you've made.

The Impact of the 12 Principles on Marriage

These 12 principles can go a long way toward saving your marriage. By following the principles, you and your spouse can enjoy more honest communication and trust, which will lead to a rebuilt intimacy. You will learn about codependent behaviors and how to break free of them. You will learn how to help your spouse, not control them. You will learn about taking personal responsibility for yourself and your actions.

Although recovery from addiction is a painful process and may at times feel as though it is tearing your marriage further apart, a couple can make it through addiction and recovery with their marriage intact and stronger than ever before.

| "Users of pornography eventually put religion, marriage, family, work and friendships secondary to their desire for pornography."

Pornography Is Addictive and Damages Relationships

Patrick A. Trueman

In the following viewpoint, Patrick A. Trueman contends that pornography is morally and spiritually offensive and is prolific among the American public. Trueman further maintains that pornography has such an addictive and dysfunctional effect on the brain that viewers eventually neglect everything else in life and cease to care about the welfare of their marriages and families. Patrick A. Trueman is president and chief executive officer of Morality in Media, a faith-based, nonprofit organization that seeks to raise awareness about the harms of pornography.

As you read, consider the following questions:

1. According to Patrick A. Trueman, why do adult pornography consumers often move on to child pornography?

2. In what ways can viewing pornography change the user's attitude toward sex and society, according to Trueman?

3. How were many pornography addicts first exposed to pornography, according to Trueman?

Pornography is now more popular than baseball. In fact, it has become America's pastime, and we are awash in it. Porn is on our computers, our smartphones, and our cable or satellite TV. It's common in our hotels and even in many retail stores and gas stations. For many men—and, increasingly, women—it is part of their daily lives.

While astounding to many, users of pornography eventually put religion, marriage, family, work and friendships secondary to their desire for pornography. They may want to change, to go back to life as it was before porn, but most will return and descend further. Dr. Mary Anne Layden, director of the University of Pennsylvania's Sexual Trauma and Psychopathology Program at the Center for Cognitive Therapy, likens pornography to crack cocaine. In a testimony to the U.S. Senate in November 2004, she noted, "This material is potent, addictive and permanently implanted in the brain."

Sadly, for the regular consumer of pornography, confession and contrition are normally not sufficient to break from pornography because, like drug abuse, pornography is not just a bad habit—it is often an addiction.

An Addiction That Does Not Satisfy

Addiction to pornography is now commonplace among adults and is even a growing problem for children and teenagers. Few who are addicted will get help, and the consequences can be lifelong and severe.

Pornography's addictive strength is a result of long-term, sometimes lifelong, neuroplastic changes in the brain. Psychiatrist Norman Doidge, author of the best-selling book *The*

Brain That Changes Itself (Penguin, 2007), writes, "Pornography, by offering an endless harem of sexual objects, hyperactivates the appetitive system. Porn viewers develop new maps in their brains, based on the photos and videos they see. Because it is a use-it-or-lose-it brain, when we develop a map area, we long to keep it activated. Just as our muscles become impatient for exercise if we've been sitting all day, so too do our senses hunger to be stimulated."

With pornography, in other words, our brain's pleasure system that excites our desires is activated, but there is no real satisfaction. This explains why users can spend endless hours searching for pornography on the Internet.

Doidge further notes that porn viewers develop tolerances so that they need higher and higher levels of stimulation. Thus, they often move to harder, more deviant pornography. More than a decade ago, Margaret A. Healy, adjunct professor at Fordham University School of Law, and Muireann O'Brian, former head of End Child Pornography, Prostitution and Trafficking (ECPAT), observed a link between adult and child pornography. Since that time, scores of current and former law enforcement authorities have noted that many adult porn consumers will eventually move to child pornography, even if they are not pedophiles and had no interest in such material at first. These findings account, in part, for the prevalence of child pornography in the world today.

Viewing porn changes the user's attitude toward sex, his or her spouse and society. He or she uses sexual fantasies to get aroused, tries to get partners to act out pornographic scenes, is more likely to engage in sexual harassment and sexual aggression, and views sex as a casual, non-intimate, recreational privilege. Layden and other clinical psychologists have reported that, ironically, erectile dysfunction is commonly associated with constant porn use among men. One reason for this is that the constant search for sexual images and often-accompanying masturbation lead to dissatisfaction with one's spouse. After all, a man's wife cannot possibly maintain an image that competes with the women in the fantasy world of pornographic videos and images. The regular porn consumer sets himself up for disappointment and the almost-certain disintegration of his marriage.

Marital love is meant to be a total giving of oneself to a lifelong, faithful partner. It is a trusting, selfless giving. By contrast, pornographic sex is selfish, demeaning and mechanical.

Protecting Our Children

A father has a duty to keep his children from pornography and a sacred obligation to set an example of purity for his family.

If you have become a porn consumer, ask yourself this: Am I the same man who professed fidelity to my wife on my wedding day? Fidelity cannot be maintained if one consumes pornography. Wives of porn consumers feel as though their husbands are committing adultery. Affairs of the mind are every bit as destructive as affairs of the heart.

Divorce lawyers report a high correspondence between pornography consumption and divorces. One 2004 study in *Social Science Quarterly* titled "Adult Social Bonds and Use of Internet Pornography" revealed that persons having an extramarital affair were more than three times more likely to have accessed Internet porn than those who did not have affairs. Further, those ever having engaged in paid sex were 3.7 times more apt to be using Internet porn than those who had not.

If you have a porn habit, your children may follow. Many pornography addicts report that their first exposure to porn was the discovery of their parent's porn collection, which started them on a life of sexual confusion and exploitation. A 2006 survey of the National Center for Missing and Exploited Children revealed that 79 percent of youth gain unwanted exposure to pornography in the home.

To a child, pornography normalizes sexual harm, according to Dr. Sharon Cooper, a pediatrician at the University of North Carolina. "Research has shown that the prefrontal cortex—the home of good judgment, common sense, impulse control and emotions—is not completely mature until children are 20–22 years of age," she explained. The introduction of pornography to the brain's prefrontal cortex is therefore devastating to key areas of a child's development and may be life-altering. "When a child sees adult pornography . . . their brains will convince them that they are actually experiencing what they are seeing," Cooper added. In other words, what a child sees in porn is what they believe is reality.

Some children will actually emulate what they see in pornography and experiment on siblings, relatives and friends. Many studies show that children exposed to pornography initiate sexual activity at an earlier age, have more sex partners, and have multiple partners in a short period of time. A 2001 study in the journal *Pediatrics* also found that teenage girls exposed to pornographic movies have sex more frequently and have a strong desire to become pregnant.

Thankfully, there are organizations, counselors and resources that provide hope for those suffering from the destructive effects of pornography on children, marriages, relationships and society. Many who have been addicted—adults and children alike—have been helped through counseling or resources offered by recovery services.

| "In every region investigated, researchers have found that as pornography has increased in availability, sex crimes have either decreased or not increased."

The Damaging Effects of Pornography Have Been Exaggerated

Milton Diamond

In the following viewpoint, Milton Diamond argues that despite claims that pornography use contributes to the degradation of women and encourages people to commit sex-related crimes, no legitimate evidence proves such claims. Diamond further asserts that statistics can be interpreted to show the use of pornography actually reduces the incidences of rape and child sex abuse. Milton Diamond is a professor at the University of Hawaii and the director of the Pacific Center for Sex and Society, a nonprofit research center at the University of Hawaii that focuses on sex as it relates to social issues.

As you read, consider the following questions:

1. Do all feminists claim that pornography denigrates women, according to Milton Diamond?

2. According to Diamond, has any US community ever voted to ban adult access to sexually explicit material?

3. Does research show that incarcerated rapists watch more pornography than nonrapists, according to Diamond?

Pornography. Most people have seen it, and have a strong opinion about it. Many of those opinions are negative—some people argue that ready access to pornography disrupts social order, encouraging people to commit rape, sexual assault, and other sex-related crimes. And even if pornography doesn't trigger a crime, they say, it contributes to the degradation of women. It harms the women who are depicted by pornography, and harms those who do not participate but are encouraged to perform the acts depicted in it by men who are acculturated by it. Many even adamantly believe that pornography should become illegal.

Alternatively, others argue that pornography is an expression of fantasies that can actually inhibit sexual activity, and act as a positive displacement for sexual aggression. Pornography offers a readily available means of satisfying sexual arousal (masturbation), they say, which serves as a substitute for dangerous, harmful, and illegal activities.

Some feminists even claim that pornography can empower women by loosening them from the shackles of social prudery and restrictions.

Facts Versus Opinions Regarding Pornography

But what do the data say? Over the years, many scientists have investigated the link between pornography (considered legal under the First Amendment in the United States unless judged "obscene") and sex crimes and attitudes towards women. And in every region investigated, researchers have found that as pornography has increased in availability, sex crimes have either decreased or not increased.

It's not hard to find a study population, given how wide-spread pornography has become. The United States alone produces 10,000 pornographic movies each year. The Free Speech Coalition, a porn industry lobbying group, estimates that adult video/DVD sales and rentals amount to at least $4 billion per year. The Internet is a rich source, with 40 million adults regularly visiting porn Web sites, and more than one-quarter of regular users downloading porn at work. And it's not just men who are interested: Nielsen/Net [an online global information and measurement company] reports that 9.4 million women in the United States accessed online pornography Web sites in the month of September 2003. According to the conservative media watchdog group Family Safe Media, the porn industry makes more money than the top technology companies combined, including Microsoft, Google, Apple, and Amazon.

No correlation has been found between exposure to porn and negative attitudes towards women.

Pornography and Sex Crimes

To examine the effect this widespread use of porn may be having on society, researchers have often exposed people to porn and measured some variable such as changes in attitude or predicted hypothetical behaviors, interviewed sex offenders about their experience with pornography, and interviewed victims of sex abuse to evaluate if pornography was involved in the assault. Surprisingly few studies have linked the availability of porn in any society with antisocial behaviors or sex crimes. Among those studies none have found a causal relationship and very few have even found one positive correlation.

Despite the widespread and increasing availability of sexually explicit materials, according to national FBI Department of Justice statistics, the incidence of rape declined markedly from 1975 to 1995. This was particularly seen in the age categories 20–24 and 25–34, the people most likely to use the In-

Public Acceptance of Pornography

In a *Christianity Today* [magazine] survey in 2000, 33% of Christian clergy admitted to having visited a sexually explicit web site. Of those who had visited a porn site, 53% had visited such sites "a few times" in the preceding year, and 18% visited sexually explicit sites from a couple of times a month to more than once a week. And it is not just men but women too who are increasingly indulging in both the use and production of porn. One study in 1989 reported that college men averaged six hours of porn viewing a month while college women averaged about two and a half hours a month. Safe Families, a Christian Internet monitoring group, reported that 34% of female readers of *Today's Christian Women's* online newsletter admitted to intentionally accessing Internet pornography. The Nielson/Net Ratings report for September 2003 stated that more than 32 million unique individuals visited a porn site in September of that year. Nearly 22.8 million of them were male (71 percent), while 9.4 million adult site visitors were female (29 percent).

Milton Diamond,
"Pornography, Public Acceptance and Sex Related Crime:
A Review," International Journal of Law and Psychiatry,
vol. 32, no. 5, September–October 2009.

ternet. The best known of these national studies are those of Berl Kutchinsky, who studied Denmark, Sweden, West Germany, and the United States in the 1970s and 1980s. He showed that for the years from approximately 1964 to 1984, as the amount of pornography increasingly became available, the rate of rapes in these countries either decreased or remained relatively level. Later research has shown parallel findings in every other country examined, including Japan, Croatia, China, Poland, Finland, and the Czech Republic. In the United States there has been a consistent decline in rape over the last 2 decades [1990–2010], and in those countries that allowed for the possession of child pornography, child sex abuse has declined. Significantly, no community in the United States has ever voted to ban adult access to sexually explicit material. The only feature of a community standard that holds is an intolerance for materials in which minors are involved as participants or consumers.

In terms of the use of pornography by sex offenders, the police sometimes suggest that a high percentage of sex offenders are found to have used pornography. This is meaningless, since most men have at some time used pornography. Looking closer, Michael Goldstein and Harold Kant [authors of the book *Pornography and Sexual Deviance*] found that rapists were more likely than nonrapists in the prison population to have been punished for looking at pornography while a youngster, while other research has shown that incarcerated nonrapists had seen more pornography, and seen it at an earlier age, than rapists. What does correlate highly with sex offense is a strict, repressive religious upbringing. . . .

No Evidence Pornography Leads to Antisocial Behavior

Now let's look at attitudes towards women. Studies of men who had seen X-rated movies found that they were significantly more tolerant and accepting of women than those men who didn't see those movies, and studies by other investigators—female as well as male—essentially found similarly that there was no detectable relationship between the amount of exposure to pornography and any measure of misogynist attitudes. No researcher or critic has found the opposite, that exposure to pornography—by any definition—has had a cause-and-effect relationship towards ill feelings or actions against women. No correlation has even been found between exposure to porn and calloused attitudes toward women.

There is no doubt that some people have claimed to suffer adverse effects from exposure to pornography—just look at testimony from women's shelters, divorce courts and other venues. But there is no *evidence* it was the *cause* of the claimed abuse or harm.

Ultimately, there is no freedom that can't be and isn't misused. This can range from the freedom to bear arms to the freedom to bear children. . . . But it doesn't mean that the freedom of the majority should be restricted to prevent the abuses of the few. When people transgress into illegal behavior, there are laws to punish them, and those act as a deterrent. In the United States, where one out of every 138 residents is incarcerated, just imagine if pornography were illegal—there'd be more people in prison than out.

> "When parents behave erratically, as in addiction, they often lose the respect of their children, who experience a corresponding loss of safety and self-esteem."

Living with Someone Who Has an Addiction

Lance Dodes

In the following viewpoint, Lance Dodes explains that children rely on their parents for a sense of safety, love, and emotional well-being; thus, when children witness one or both parents behaving erratically, angrily, or dishonestly, their peace of mind is shattered. Dodes further maintains that older children and adolescents suffer a greater loss than young children because they cannot count on their addicted parents to provide the sound advice and support that they need as they are maturing. Lance Dodes is a training and supervising analyst with the Boston Psychoanalytic Society and Institute and an assistant clinical professor of psychiatry at Harvard Medical School. He is the author of The Heart of Addiction *and* Breaking Addiction: A 7-Step Handbook for Ending Any Addiction, *from which this viewpoint is excerpted.*

As you read, consider the following questions:

1. According to Lance Dodes, should parents allow their very young children to witness their out-of-control behaviors?

2. Should parents discuss their own behavior with their children, according to Dodes?

3. According to Dodes, is it a good idea for a parent to reassure a child that the addictive behavior will never happen again?

Depending on the age of the child, addiction in a parent may mean anything from a fundamental loss of safety to the loss of the child's sense of his or her own value.

The Meaning of Addiction to Very Young Children

When addiction is visible to a very young child, as when a parent is drunk or high at home, it can be a very frightening experience. Children need to have—and assume that their parents are—powerful figures who are able to protect them. Parents are seen as capable of controlling the very young child's world. This sometimes leads to disappointment in parents when adverse events occur: a party that is rained out is cause to feel cheated by Mom and Dad, who should have controlled the weather ("But you promised!"). It is likewise taken for granted that parents can control themselves. They are omnipotent beings and need to be, to keep the child safe.

In this context, a parent who is clearly out of control of himself is a blow to a child's normal sense of safety. It is not Mommy or Daddy who is out of control; it is the world. Therefore, it is important that parents appreciate the extent of the fear such out-of-control behavior can create in their child. In talking with the child it is necessary to reassure him or her that both parents are still in control of the child's world. This may be far more important than, for instance, apologizing to the young child, or explaining the basis for the parent's behavior. The effects on very young children also underscore the importance of keeping out-of-control behavior out of their sight as much as possible.

The Meaning of Addiction to Older Children and Adolescents

As a child grows, a parent's addiction shifts from producing global fear of a chaotic world to producing attempts to decipher the meaning of a parent's problem. An older child is also able to recognize a broader spectrum of addictive behavior. Gambling, binge eating, and other compulsive or addictive behaviors may now also be seen as indicators of a parent's loss of control.

The effects of a parent's addiction on an older child depend on the child's relationship with his parent, and the parents' ability to keep up healthy two-way communication with their child, allowing them to hear the child's thoughts and feelings so he does not have to be alone with his worries (which may be distorted and inflated compared to the real possibilities).

The Effects of a Parent's Addiction on a Child's Respect and Self-Respect

All children, for their sense of safety and emotional well-being, need to be able to respect their parents. Parents who are respected enable children to feel safe because they believe their parents can be relied upon. And since children identify with their parents, seeing them in a positive light enables children to feel valuable themselves. This is especially true when children are younger, but continues through adolescence, although in the teenage years the importance of identification with parents is often masked by the normal rebelliousness of that age. Adolescents who say that they couldn't care less about what their parents are like are saying this because they are in the process of defining their own identities apart from their parents. But as long as they are not yet fully grown, that claim cannot be taken at face value, and the way parents behave is still important to their sense of themselves.

When parents behave erratically, as in addiction, they often lose the respect of their children, who experience a corresponding loss of safety and self-esteem. We, as adults with understanding of the nature of addiction, don't lose our respect for people suffering with addictions. But young people are not in that position. They have all the misperceptions about addiction that adults have had through the ages: that it is a sign of weakness, immorality, selfishness, and lack of caring or concern for others. These feelings may be expressed openly or kept secret. Older children and adolescents will often express themselves openly. With younger or less verbal children, the same feelings are likely present, however, so with them it takes a special attentiveness and ongoing acceptance of their feelings to help them express what they are secretly thinking. Either way, the task is to explain the nature of addiction in terms accessible to the child, with the goal of helping the child understand addiction as a sign of upset feelings in the parent who has addiction, and as a condition that has nothing to do with morality, weakness, or their love for their child.

It is also critical to let the child know that his anger, disappointment, and sadness are perfectly normal and completely justified. A child may have trouble with the duality of understanding both that the parent is suffering with a problem and that the child has every right to have her feelings, especially her anger. Even adults can have trouble with this. . . . People often think in terms of right and wrong, good and bad, making it hard to understand and value the feelings of both parties in a conflictual relationship. When it comes to children and their parents this is especially hard. Children want their parents to be good, wise, and strong. If they view their parents as lacking in these qualities it can throw them into turmoil. As a solution, to preserve that needed sense of a parent's goodness, children may instead blame themselves for problems. This may take the form of literally blaming themselves for the parent's behavior: "If only I hadn't made Daddy so upset he wouldn't have gotten drunk." Or, more insidiously, children may blame themselves for their angry feelings: "I must be a bad person to think such mad thoughts about Mommy." Either way, it is important to listen for these feelings in your child and to reassure him about them. A mother might say to her son, "If my mother did what I did, I'd be angry with her too. Actually, I am angry with me. We're both upset about what I did. Let's be sure we keep talking about how we both feel about me when I do things like that."

The Effects of a Parent's Addiction on a Child's Trust

Trusting parents overlaps with respecting them, of course. Just like adults, children lose respect for untrustworthy people, including their parents. There is also another issue with untrustworthiness. Once parents are deemed untrustworthy they are less likely to be approached for help or guidance. In the case of addictions, this means children may be less willing or able to listen to your explanations of the problem.

Younger children in particular may take your untrustworthiness in one instance—such as saying you won't repeat an addictive behavior—as evidence that you are untrustworthy in general. Consequently, it is wise to adhere to the following rule:

> Never tell a child (or adolescent or adult for that matter) that an addictive behavior—on your part or the part of your spouse—will never happen again. That sort of promise, even though it is tempting to make in the moment in order to help the child feel better, is a disappointment waiting to happen.

But even saying that you will try your hardest to stop is easily heard as a promise by children. After all, you are a powerful figure to a young child and if you say you'll try your hardest, she will assume that you will succeed. So, when talking to your child it is better to describe how difficult it is for you (or your spouse) to manage the feelings that lead to addictive behavior. You can certainly add that you or your spouse is trying to control it, but to avoid disappointing her or losing her trust, you should go out of your way to explain that the behavior is likely to continue for a while, at least. If the behavior then does not diminish, it will be important to be open with your child about that, too. This will help lessen feelings that he or she has been lied to, and help the child express his or her own feelings of frustration and sadness. . . .

Older children and adolescents are less likely to globalize a lack of trust and more likely to see the problem as separate from other areas of the parent's trustworthiness. For them, the bigger problem may be that they can't turn to the parent with addiction for advice. This might be expressed as, "Why should I ask you about how to do anything, you can't even control your own life!" Certainly, this involves loss of respect for the parent whose overall value is seen as tarnished, but there is a more specific sense that views about life from this parent cannot be trusted. Since children and adolescents regularly need help in making decisions, this is a real loss for them. Young people regularly turn to each other for advice and information about difficult decisions—sometimes with bad results—and they are likely to do this even more if they feel their parents are not trustworthy guides.

As with younger children, honesty and openness are crucial in maintaining, or rebuilding, your child's trust. As they grow older, children idealize their parents less, and can better appreciate hearing of the struggle with addiction that parents are going through. It is helpful to adopt an open attitude that says, "I'm having an awful time trying to control this addiction, and I know it's hard on you and the family. But I'm still your father/mother. I've still lived a lot of life, and I'm not dumb. I can still give you some good advice about things or help you to think about your problems. Just don't ask me when I'm upset/drunk/bingeing. And I'll try not to give you advice when I'm in that state, either!"

Special Consideration When Discussing Addiction with Young Children

When discussing addiction with your child, and listening to your child's concerns, keep in mind that his fears and anxieties may be distorted and extreme compared to your own way of thinking. For example, when a small child's father is drunk, or secluded in a room watching a sports event on which he has a bet, the child may tell you that his father hates him—or even wants to kill him. Perhaps you're prepared for the child's notion that his father is angry with him, but his fear of being murdered may well come as a surprise. Yet, such thoughts are commonplace in young children, for whom primal feelings are close to the surface. In other cases, a child might interpret a parent's behavior as suicidal, or express thoughts about harming the parent or parts of the parent's body. Or children may include the entire world in their thinking. The world will end, or monsters will eat the house, the child, or a parent. Mostly, as you can see, these thoughts suggest the fear and aggression with which the child is living. But they also may have a distinctly depressive quality. Fearing the end of the world can suggest a child's sense of some imminent catastrophe, but it can also refer to her loneliness and despair. It is important to try to hear whatever feelings your child is conveying in her own manner.

By talking with your child about her feelings and correcting your child's disproportionate fears, you reinforce her sense of security, and disconnect her feelings from the scary ideas she has invented.

> "Not only do batterers tend to abuse
> drugs and alcohol, but the probability
> that victims of domestic violence will
> turn to alcohol and drugs to cope with
> the abuse increases as well."

Substance Abuse Can Lead to Family Violence

Addiction Treatment Magazine

In the following viewpoint, Addiction Treatment Magazine, *an online magazine that focuses on all types of addiction and treatment options, contends that domestic violence is a hidden fallout of substance abuse and becomes more frequent and severe over time. According to the magazine, perpetrators are usually men, and their targets of violence include spouses, partners, children, siblings, and even elderly relatives.* Addiction Treatment Magazine *further contends that substance-abusing batterers must undergo simultaneous treatment for their drug abuse and their violent urges. Treating only the substance abuse will not stop the violence.*

As you read, consider the following questions:

1. According to *Addiction Treatment Magazine,* are women who have been targets of substance-abuse-related violence more or less likely to abuse alcohol or drugs themselves?

2. After the substance abusing batterer completes treatment for substance abuse, does the domestic abuse generally stop, according to *Addiction Treatment Magazine?*

3. In some cases, is the family able to overcome substance abuse and domestic violence without outside support, according to *Addiction Treatment Magazine?*

How well do we really know our neighbors? Hidden behind closed doors, all kinds of physical and emotional abuse occur at the hands of spouses or partners, parents and others living in the home. Most often, it's the wife and children who suffer the consequences of a spouse and father (or male residing with them).

While substance abuse does not cause domestic violence, say the experts, there is a statistical correlation between the two issues. What studies of domestic violence have found is that there is frequent high incidence of alcohol and other drug use by perpetrators during domestic abuse. The reality is that not only do batterers tend to abuse drugs and alcohol, but the probability that victims of domestic violence will turn to alcohol and drugs to cope with the abuse increases as well.

The Facts About Domestic Violence and Substance Abuse

Delving into what's known about the two issues—domestic violence and substance abuse—can shed some light on the problem that affects so many in America.

- Regular alcohol abuse is one of the leading risk factors for partner violence (between spouses or partners).

- When there is a battering incident coupled with alcohol abuse, the battering may be more severe and result in greater injury to the victim or victims.

- Studies of alcoholic women indicate that they are more likely to report they've had childhood physical and emotional abuse than women who are nonalcoholic.

- In fact, women who have been abused are 15 times more likely to abuse alcohol and nine times more likely to abuse drugs than women who have not been abused.

- Relative to the type of childhood abuse suffered, the National Center on Addiction and Substance Abuse found that 69 percent of women being treated for substance abuse reported they were sexually abused as children.

- Treatment for alcoholism does not cure abusive behavior.

- The Department of Justice found in 2002 that 36 percent of victims in domestic violence programs also had problems with substance abuse.

- According to a majority of domestic violence program directors (51 percent), a woman's use of alcohol can be a barrier to her being able to leave a violent relationship with a spouse or partner.

- An even greater percentage (87 percent) of domestic violence program directors agree with the statement that the risk of intimate partner violence increases when both partners abuse drugs or alcohol.

Domestic Violence—What It Is

Domestic violence is the intentional use of physical, emotional, psychological, or sexual force by one family member—or intimate partner—to control another.

The form domestic violence takes includes acts of:

- Intimidation—physical, emotional and verbal

- Threats

- Forced sex

- Killing or maiming pets

- Destruction of family members' property or possessions

- Slapping, punching, choking, kicking, burning, stabbing victims

- Killing victims

Targets of domestic violence include spouses, intimate partners, parents, stepparents, children, stepchildren, siblings, and elderly relatives.

In the United States, a woman is beaten every 15 seconds. Thirty percent of trauma patients (excluding victims of traffic accidents) are victims of domestic violence. The medical costs associated with treating women who have been victims of domestic violence at the hands of their partners is $44 million each year.

In eight to 13 percent of all marriages, severe physical assaults of women occur. The assaults reoccur in two-thirds of those relationships.

Similar to the patterns of substance abuse, domestic violence tends to increase in frequency and severity over time.

Men as Batterers

Men are generally considered to be the stronger sex, particularly in terms of physical strength. But this also often means they inflict profound and lasting emotional damage on their spouses and children.

Batterers who abuse alcohol and are living with women often try to justify their violent actions as a way to control their victims when they are drunk. They also use alcohol as an excuse for the violence, blaming what they've done on alcohol. This way, they avoid taking responsibility for their actions. At least, they attempt to rid themselves of the onus by making statements like this: "I didn't do it—it was the alcohol! I'd never hurt you, you know that."

When batterers cause substantial injury to their victims and wind up in jail, some of the statistics revealed can be shocking.

The U.S. Department of Justice (DOJ) found that 61 percent of domestic violence offenders also have substance abuse problems. An early (1994) study on murder in families conducted by the DOJ found that more than half of the defendants accused of murdering their spouses were drinking alcohol at the time of the violent incident.

The Battered Woman's Reality

A battered woman literally lives in a war zone. She never knows what's going to trigger a violent outburst from her spouse or partner. There may be subtle signs of an impending abusive incident, but often there are none.

She tries to read her partner for any such indications, watching his every move, facial expression, listens to his tone of voice, trying to interpret what's going on in his head. Searching for behavior cues and indicators of changing moods takes a lot of time and energy, and she's not always successful.

Unable to, or afraid that she won't be able to, support herself and her children on her own, along with constant fear that her spouse will make good on his threats to harm family members, the battered woman stays in the home. As such, she's likely to fear her batterer will continue to stalk and harass her, possibly even kill her.

In many instances, the batterer also serves as the woman's supplier of drugs and/or alcohol. This compounds the problem of the woman leaving. Being so dependent on the spouse or partner for financial as well as drug supplies, the woman often becomes so damaged emotionally as well as physically that she simply cannot imagine being able to make it on her own.

Children in Abusive Homes

Perhaps the most heartbreaking consequence of the dual issues of domestic violence and substance abuse is what happens to the children involved. Instead of being nurtured, children living in abusive homes where drugs and alcohol abuse occur simultaneously are often deprived of more than just the basics of food and shelter. They may face lifelong consequences resulting from parents who abuse substances and resort to violence. . . .

There is also evidence that children who run away to escape violence at home are at risk of developing substance abuse. Again, it's often a matter of coping with the pain, trying to block out the memories.

What Victims Need to Know

There's no question that the victims of domestic violence and substance abuse have a difficult situation. Often they don't know where to turn or are fearful of letting anyone outside the home know of the violence and abuse. If they say anything, they may suffer even worse at the hands of the substance abusing batterer. In the face of such fear, they often continue to suffer in silence.

The batterers often exhibit profound remorse over what they've done, promising to never do it again, blaming the alcohol or drugs. But the truth is that domestic violence never just goes away. And it won't stop just because the person doing the battering stops using alcohol or drugs.

Even when the substance abusing batterer goes into treatment for substance abuse, treatment for that alone will not curtail the abuse. Both need to be treated simultaneously. Unfortunately, too many people believe that it's just the drugs or alcohol that causes the violence. The tragic result is that the batterer, once rehab is complete, still has the underlying psychological impulse to abuse his (or her) spouse and/or children. Without treatment to overcome those urges, the violence will simply continue. The bottom line is that one problem (substance abuse or domestic violence) cannot be addressed without also dealing with the other.

While it's understandable that victims of domestic violence and substance abuse would seek a way out of the pain, attempting to cope by using drugs or alcohol cannot only defeat the purpose, it can have lasting and profound consequences. It can lead to further problems such as drug and alcohol dependency and the potential for increased vulnerability to violence. Besides alcohol and illicit drugs, abuse of prescription drugs such as tranquilizers, sedatives, stimulants and painkillers can lead to dependency.

There's not going to be any effective support inside the home for overcoming the dual issues of substance abuse and domestic violence. The barriers to surmount are simply too high and family members—those who are the victims—are not equipped to deal with them. Protection, support, and treatment have to come from outside the family, in almost every instance. . . .

Treatment for Substance-Abusing Batterers

Similar to individuals seeking treatment for substance abuse, when a person enters treatment for substance abuse who is a batterer, he or she is likely in a crisis state. He may have been referred to the treatment program by the courts after being arrested for drug- or violence-related charges. He may have been left alone by his partner and children after they sought safety from his physical and emotional violence. In any case, the danger of violence erupting is always present.

Fostering accountability is of vital importance in successful treatment. Experts say that the degree to which a batterer begins to assume responsibility for his actions can serve as a barometer for his progress during substance abuse treatment.

Referral to and collaboration with batterer intervention programs can help facilitate treatment for substance abuse in batterers. The relationship between substance abuse and violent behavior needs to be examined. Answers to the following questions can help treatment providers prepare an appropriate treatment plan:

- Exactly when, in relation to an instance of substance abuse, does the violence occur?

- How much of the violent behavior occurs when the individual is drinking or using drugs?

- What substances are used before the violent act?

- What feelings precede or accompany the use of drugs or alcohol?

- Is alcohol or drugs used to recover from an incident of violence?

Other areas of treatment typically include bonding with peers and parenting classes. There is also a focus on the matter of ongoing support for the substance-abusing batterers. While there are many national 12-step groups for those in recovery from alcohol, drugs, gambling, compulsive sexual behavior and other disorders, there are no ongoing organizations that support change for men who batter, nor their surviving victims. . . .

Bringing the Hidden Problem to Light

Shining a spotlight on domestic violence, the hidden side of substance abuse, isn't easy. The victims are understandably reticent about coming forward. Fearing for their safety, they may be unwilling or unable to get treatment or help for themselves. Batterers who also abuse substances are unlikely to be forthcoming about their violent behavior. But the prevalence of domestic violence and substance abuse in today's society necessitates continued intervention, prevention, treatment and recovery services.

Periodical and Internet Sources Bibliography

The following articles have been selected to supplement the diverse views presented in this chapter.

Lauren Dubinsky "What I Wish I'd Known Before Watching Porn," *The Huffington Post*, July 23, 2012.

Peter Ferentzy "Tough Love Is a Joke—Let's Start Enabling Drug Addicts Everywhere," *The Huffington Post*, October 10, 2011.

Mohamed Ghilan "How Watching Pornography Changes the Brain," SuhaibWebb.com, January 23, 2012.

Elizabeth Hartney "Connections Between Substance Use and Family Violence," About.com, July 15, 2011.

Melinda Wenner Moyer "The Sunny Side of Smut," *Scientific American*, July 22, 2011.

Erica Orloff "Can Marriage Survive Addiction?" Full Spectrum Recovery and Counseling.

Celia Vimont "Jerry Moe: Call for More Research on Parent's Addiction Recovery and Its Effect on Children," The Partnership at Drugfree.org, October 4, 2011.

Naomi Wolf "The Porn Myth," *New York*, November 4, 2012.

Jazmine Woodberry "More than the Bottle: How Other Addictions Affect College Students," *Daily Wildcat*, April 29, 2012.

How Can Addictions Be Treated?

Chapter Preface

In 1971 US president Richard Nixon declared a "war on drugs," leading an effort to discourage the production, distribution, and consumption of illegal drugs. The government's efforts, however, were unsuccessful. In June 2011 the Global Commission on Drug Policy released a critical report, declaring "the global war on drugs has failed, with devastating consequences for individuals and societies around the world." In fact, in the early twenty-first century, more drug use occurred in North America than ever before. Since the 1990s, the percentage of high school seniors who smoke marijuana daily has more than doubled, as has the rate of death from drug overdose among Americans between the ages of fifteen and twenty-four. And studies by the National Center on Addiction and Substance Abuse at Columbia University (CASAColumbia) found that 80 percent of felony inmates and juveniles in legal custody are influenced in some way by drug or alcohol addiction. Retired detective Lieutenant Jack A. Cole of the New Jersey State Police Department believes that legalizing drugs would be one way to successfully treat drug abuse and addiction. He says, "We legalize all drugs—legalize them so we can regulate and control them and keep them out of the hands of our children." More and more experts and researchers are starting to agree with Cole and contend that the United States should vigorously pursue such an approach. In 2012, Colorado and Washington took action in this direction by repealing laws against the recreational use of marijuana.

For example, in 2002, five former police officers, including retired Michigan detective Howard Wooldridge, created the nonprofit organization Law Enforcement Against Prohibition (LEAP). In his book, *Smoke Signals: A Social History of Marijuana—Medical, Recreational, and Scientific*, Martin A. Lee describes the group:

LEAP [grew] into a 40,000 member international organization composed of former prosecutors, undercover narcotics agents, judges, prison wardens, constables, and other disillusioned government functionaries who, after years of toiling in the trenches of a conflict with no conceivable end, had come to view the war on drugs as a colossal failure that fostered crime, police corruption, social discord, racial injustice, and, ironically, drug abuse itself, while squandering billions of tax dollars, clogging courtrooms and prisons, weakening constitutional safeguards, and impeding medical advances.... Wooldridge called it "the most dysfunctional, immoral domestic policy since slavery and Jim Crow."

The mission of LEAP is to reform drug laws so that the sale and distribution of drugs would be regulated by a government body. "The benefit to the drug addict would be huge. Getting his drugs from a legal source would access him to counseling, support, therapy—all the things he or she needs to break dependency," explains Edward Ellison, former drugs squad chief of the Metropolitan Police Service in London, England.

Many people, however, do not want to be seen as tolerant of drug addicts or as soft on criminals. Others fear that legalizing drugs will lead to widespread substance use among young people and greater dependency, addiction, and treatment costs—a fear that is not supported by the evidence. According to a 2001 survey conducted in Holland, where drugs are basically legal, 28 percent of tenth graders had used marijuana compared to a much higher 41 percent of tenth graders in the United States.

Supporters of the legalization of drugs insist that treating drug addicts as criminals is not effective policy. "We need to absorb in our minds and guts the utter futility of what we are doing now," writes physician and addiction expert Gabor Maté in his book, *In the Realm of Hungry Ghosts: Close Encounters with Addiction*. Former drug addict and author Tony O'Neill agrees with Maté. In an article for the addiction and recovery website The Fix, O'Neill writes, "The addiction community's number one priority has to be convincing the powers that be to end drug prohibition. Only when drug use is classified as a medical rather than a legal issue can resources finally be focused."

| "We, as humans, are physiologically pat-
terned to resonate to each other at a
deep neural level through a phenomenon called limbic resonance."

Twelve-Step Programs Help Heal the Emotional Pain of Addiction

Tian Dayton

*In the following viewpoint, Tian Dayton explains that the com-
radeship and emotional connection with other people that twelve-
step meetings provide soothe the addicted body's limbic system.
Dayton further maintains that the healing energy of twelve-step
groups gradually helps the addict build new trustworthy relationships and eventually will lessen the trauma of living as an
addict. Tian Dayton is a clinical psychologist and the author of
the books* Emotional Sobriety: From Relationship Trauma to
Resilience and Balance, *and* Trauma and Addiction: Ending
the Cycle of Pain Through Emotional Literacy.

As you read, consider the following questions:

1. Are human beings physiologically patterned to empa-
   thize with other people, according to Tian Dayton?

2. Since it is developed throughout childhood, can the brain's limbic system be reprogrammed in adulthood, according to Dayton?

3. What parts of daily life does the limbic system govern, according to Dayton?

Why do people feel better after attending a twelve step meeting? Why do twelve step meetings work so well for healing emotional pain and establishing new behaviors? Some of that answer lies in neurobiology. Because of the way our nervous systems are put together, going to meetings can actually restructure our limbic systems.

The Phenomenon of Limbic Resonance

We, as humans, are physiologically patterned to resonate to each other at a deep neural level through a phenomenon called limbic resonance. Like it or not, we are wired to pick up on and process other people's emotions through our own neurological networks. Daniel Stern, an American scientist working at the University of Geneva has long been exploring these subtle interactions. "Our nervous systems" says Stern, "are constructed to be captured by the nervous systems of others, so that we can experience others as if from within their skin." Thomas Lewis, author of *A General Theory of Love* says, "Our neural architecture places relationships at the crux of our lives, where, blazing and warm, they have the power to stabilize. When people are hurting and out of balance, they turn to regulating affiliations: groups, clubs, pets, marriages, friendships, masseuses, chiropractors, the Internet. All carry at least the potential for emotional connection. Together those bonds do more good than all the psychotherapies on the planet." He goes on to connect parenting with emotional stability and strength, "A parent who rejects a child's desire to depend raises a fragile person. Those children, grown into adulthood, are frequently those who come for help."

A Beneficial Alliance

Self-help groups can complement and extend the effects of professional treatment. The most prominent self-help groups are those affiliated with Alcoholics Anonymous (AA), Narcotics Anonymous (NA), and Cocaine Anonymous (CA); all of which are based on the 12-step model. Most drug addiction treatment programs encourage patients to participate in self-help group therapy during and after formal treatment. These groups can be particularly helpful during recovery, offering an added layer of community-level social support to help people achieve and maintain abstinence and other healthy lifestyle behaviors over the course of a lifetime.

National Institute on Drug Abuse,
Principles of Drug Addiction Treatment:
A Research-Based Guide, 3rd ed. Rockville, MD:
National Institute on Drug Abuse, 2012.

The relational patterns encoded into the limbic system do not necessarily respond to insight alone. Instead they respond to the slow re-patterning or recoding of the complex brain and body systems.

Twelve-Step Programs Help Develop Emotional Regulation

Twelve step programs offer the opportunity to revise and re-pattern one's limbic system. Simply to experience powerful emotions in the presence of others and get from the beginning to the end of them without acting out or triggering a crisis or collapsing into helplessness is re-patterning and re-wiring. Slowly, over time, it re-regulates our own emotional responses, which in turn re-regulate behavior.

So how does that happen? As we sit in twelve step meetings listening to others share their "stories" in feeling ways, we come close to each other's "limbic worlds." We sit, we are stirred emotionally, we listen, we identify or notice that we do not identify. We neither affirm nor deny what is said nor do we shout back, give advice, attack or run out the door. We're aware of feelings long forgotten, we experience their effect on us, we have insights and "aha's." Over time, as this process repeats and repeats itself, something within us shifts into a more aware and understanding position. As this process, quiet on the outside but often noisy on the inside reoccurs countless times, we slowly become different on the inside, we actually learn how to feel our feelings and translate them into words, we learn to "sit with" our powerful emotions without acting out, blowing up or imploding. We develop the skills of emotional regulation. Gradually we feel more whole, capable and confident; we become capable of feeling our own feelings and thinking our own thoughts, a hallmark of independence.

Our animal brain is part of what is referred to as our "limbic system" or that part of our brain/body network that governs moods, controls appetite and sleep cycles, promotes bonding, stores highly charged emotional memories, modulates motivation, and directly processes the sense of smell and libido. In short, our limbic system is central to how we feel, sleep, eat, operate in the world and relate to others. Our limbic systems are slowly nurtured and developed throughout childhood. A well-regulated limbic system can allow us to live in balance, relate in balance, eat in balance, sleep in balance and feel in balance. Deregulation in the limbic system can lead to depression, anxiety, sleep disturbances to name a few. Also addictions can reflect problems with limbic regulation. We can have trouble regulating, for example, our relationship with alcohol, food or sex. We over do or we under do.

Twelve-Step Meetings Help Addicts Reconnect with Others

Healing emotional trauma takes time because emotions are stored in the limbic system which is in our bodies. Healing emotions therefore means neurological healing, it's healing the body.

Those who do poorly in healing deep emotional wounds in my experience are often the ones who, for some reason or another, don't like the idea of putting in the hours; the ones who want the grand "aha" the quick fix, the flash of insight that will take all their pain away. Forever. And NOW. Maybe they go to twelve step meetings and are bothered by what people do or don't say, maybe the idea of groups annoys, threatens or makes them feel vulnerable. Or perhaps a one-to-one relationship brings up more fear and mistrust than they can face feeling. But sooner or later they will need to come to terms with their aversion to connection and join something. If the trauma has been living with addiction, abuse or neglect twelve step rooms have the advantage of teaching about the disease of addiction and its long term effects. Even if addiction was a generation away the traumatic effects of living with it may still be reverberating a generation later. A parent who was raised by an alcoholic, in other words, may parent in ways that directly relate to growing up with addiction. For example, a child who felt abandoned by an alcoholic mother may be over-controlling and clinging of her children or the father who was "jerked around" by his alcoholic father may be distant or cold to his own son.

Unfortunately when it is relationships that have hurt us we can become fearful of entering the kinds of healing relationships that we need to become healthy and more balanced. The idea of dependency on others or being emotionally vulnerable in their presence brings up anxiety, resentment and fear of being disappointed or let down. It becomes fraught with fear and mistrust. Therefore, instead of being able to enter into a trusting and balanced sort of dependency, those who have been hurt in relationships may avoid emotional intimacy and closeness, because unconsciously they fear being hurt again. Twelve step rooms let them take baby steps toward a new way of relating. In the rooms they can depend on the program and the healing energy of the group rather than any one person. This less threatening form of dependency can lead them gradually toward increased trust and more manageable and meaningful connection with others.

> "*Choice, free will, the ability to script our own destiny, this is where the power—our power and the power to reclaim ourselves from our consumptive compulsions—lies.*"

Twelve-Step Programs Do Not Heal Addiction

Michael J. Formica

In the following viewpoint, Michael J. Formica contends that abiding by the underlying premise of all twelve-step recovery programs that the addict is powerless actually makes it impossible for an addict to recover. He argues that the only way for a person to achieve personal transformation is to accept responsibility for his or her behavior; in other words, become personally powerful, not powerless. Michael J. Formica is a psychotherapist, teacher, and writer with professional experience in the areas of conflict resolution, child development, and motivational behavior.

As you read, consider the following questions:

1. According to Michael J. Formica, what is the historical success rate of twelve-step programs?

2. Does free will play any part in a person's ability to recover from addiction, according to Formica?

3. Do people need to rely on external influences in order
to succeed at addiction recovery, according to Formica?

One of the central facets of addiction is the unwillingness
to take responsibility. Without exercising the all-
important watershed of self-responsibility, breaking the compulsive cycle that leads to addictive behavior is all but impossible. Systems like AA [Alcoholics Anonymous, a support
group for recovering alcoholics] or the Minnesota Model [a
prevention program consistent with the philosophies of AA],
which allow the abdication of self-responsibility to The Program, The Meeting, The Sponsor and even God, are, from this
perspective, clearly suspect and, as the numbers bear out, considerably—and understatedly—less than successful.

Twelve-Step Programs Have
Low Success Rates

In this moment, the heads of 12 Step proponents are explod-
ing, for I have blasphemed. Before you do explode, however,
consider that, if you have maintained some semblance of sobriety for any extended period coincident to participating in a
12 Step-type program, you constitute less than 5% of all those
who entered into that program within the 12 month period of
your initial participation, and 95% of your brethren left that
program sometime in those same 12 months. Given that the
Harvard Medical School reports spontaneous remission of alcoholic behavior at 50%, rethinking the Holy Grail of AA and
its sister systems, with their historically less than 5% success
rate, might be worthwhile.

One of the core elements that inform our humanity is free
will. When you were a child, the fastest way to get you to do
something was to tell you not to do it, right? Has that really
changed? If we consider driving rules as a metaphor for the

similarly hard and fast rule set fostered by the Twelve Step contingent, what we find is that, by and large, we drive over the speed limit, we don't wear our seat belts all the time, we text and talk on the cell phone while driving, and we park where we're not supposed to park, sometimes even in the handicapped zone.

Think about that for a moment. The potential legal and financial consequences of that errant behavior are even more immediate than those of going on a run. So, what makes you think that the 12 Step template has any more influence in keeping you on the straight and narrow? Jamming a rigid behavioral template down onto a creature whose primary motivations are driven by free will is, by definition, a fool's errand. Why? Because what it comes down to is choice, and choice is an interior process.

Personal Power Is Important

We cannot enter into any process of personal transformation without releasing our reliance on externals. Holding onto those externals enslaves us every bit as much as our addictions, our assumptions, our expectations, our model of the world and even our own self-perception might enslave us. As soon as we say, "I am powerless," that's exactly what we are—powerless. Choice, free will, the ability to script our own destiny, this is where the power—our power and the power to reclaim ourselves from our consumptive compulsions—lies.

In all the years that I have personally lived and worked with addicts, whether as a friend, a professional, an educator or a spiritual teacher, I have not once witnessed someone come to their sobriety—or at the very least some semblance of that sobriety—without first saying, "I just don't want to be that person any more." Granted, this observation is anecdotal, but it speaks to the very essence of choice; choice driven by a willingness to change, which, in turn, drives interior transformation and, ultimately, the reclamation of personal power.

The choice "not to be that person any more" is at the core of self-responsibility. It is the quantum moment when a person re-defines themselves on their own terms and does so by taking hold of both their life and their personal experience of the world. From this viewpoint, the 12 Step model does not afford the necessary venue for the reclamation of self and personal power because it forces us into an unrelenting system of external compliance that is anathema to the very free will that defines us.

> *"Many pharmaceutical companies have traditionally shied away from medications development for illicit drug disorders because of a relatively small patient population who also tend to be in lower income brackets."*

Pharmaceuticals and Vaccines May Help Treat Addiction

Nora D. Volkow

In the following viewpoint, Nora D. Volkow explains how scientific research has revealed addiction to be a disease of the brain, which in turn offers possible new approaches to prevent and treat drug abuse. Volkow further contends that pharmaceutical companies must work together with scientists and the medical community for this new knowledge to help end the disease of addiction. Nora D. Volkow is the director of the National Institute on Drug Abuse, an agency of the US Department of Health and Human Services that aims to disseminate scientific research to improve the prevention and treatment of drug abuse and addiction.

As you read, consider the following questions:

1. According to Nora D. Volkow, genes are responsible for what percentage of the risk for becoming addicted?

Nora D. Volkow, "Treating Addiction as a Disease: The Promise of Medication-Assisted Recovery," www.drugabuse.gov, June 23, 2010, National Institute on Drug Abuse.

2. Does the development of drug addiction vaccines offer great financial incentives for pharmaceutical companies, according to Volkow?

3. According to Volkow, would drug addiction treatment for incarcerated individuals have an effect on prison populations?

We have a public health mandate to stop the devastating scourge of drug abuse and addiction afflicting this country, and new medications to treat addiction could go a long way to achieving this end. It is a gaping need. A recent report from HHS's [the US Department of Health and Human Services] Centers for Disease Control and Prevention finds that drug-induced deaths, mainly from opioid pain reliever overdose, more than tripled from 4,000 in 1999 to 13,800 in 2006. And cigarettes continue to kill roughly 440,000 people each year in this country—yet the quest to discover treatments for nicotine addiction lags behind the efforts to develop medications for the diseases it causes. From 1987 to 2008, 174 medications trials were done for smoking cessation (46 supported by industry), compared with 1,490 clinical trials for lung cancer treatment (544 supported by industry). The possibilities present in the knowledge we have accumulated, if translated into new medications today, could transform the way we treat addiction and even how we prevent drug abuse from occurring in the first place.

Science has shown, beyond a reasonable doubt, that addiction is a disease of the brain and that our genes contribute close to half of the risk for becoming addicted. Addiction results from profound disruptions in the function of specific neurotransmitters and brain circuits. It involves an expanding cycle of dysfunction, first in the areas of the brain that process

- complex cognitive functions, such as learning (memory, reward, followed by alterations in: conditioning, habits);

- executive function (impulse inhibition, decision making, delayed gratification);

- cognitive awareness (interoception); and

- emotional functions (mood, stress reactivity).

New Knowledge Presents Possibilities for New Medications

This knowledge and other discoveries have given us numerous molecules and circuits that could serve as the basis for new approaches to medications development. Medications that target systems common to multiple addictions (e.g., stress-induced relapse) could widen the market for addiction medications and compel greater interest from pharmaceutical companies. In fact, the current pipeline of smart pharmacotherapeutic strategies embodies the translational potential of what we now know about addiction. For example:

Addiction vaccines. Vaccination is a centuries-old strategy in which the body is coaxed into producing antibodies that neutralize disease-causing agents (e.g., viruses, parasites, toxins). The concept behind this classic form of immunotherapy has only recently been explored and shown to be viable for treating addiction. In this case, antibodies are generated to specific abused drugs to bind the drug while it is still in the bloodstream, thereby reducing its entry into the central nervous system and blocking its pharmacological/behavioral effects. This approach, applied so far against nicotine and cocaine, has shown considerable promise. NicVAX, a nicotine vaccine developed by Nabi Biopharmaceuticals, is now in Phase III clinical trials for drug approval owing in part to NIDA [National Institute on Drug Abuse] support using American Reinvestment and Recovery Act funds. Although not yet approved by the U.S. Food and Drug Administration (FDA) for safety and efficacy, preliminary results show that smokers who achieved high antibody levels had higher rates of quitting and longer stretches of abstinence than those given placebo (18% vs. 6% complete abstinence after 52 weeks). The vaccine was also well tolerated, with few side effects; and it reduced craving and withdrawal symptoms, which often prompt relapse.

Long Acting (Depot) Medications (e.g., Vivitrol—injectable naltrexone currently prescribed for alcoholism). Recent clinical trials of Vivitrol for opioid dependence have produced spectacular results showing this compound could be of great help in situations where opiate replacement therapy is rejected or when the patients are hard to reach, because long-acting, or depot, medications have effects that last for weeks instead of hours and therefore promote adherence. Here, too, these results are under review by the FDA, but the drug is not yet approved for safety and efficacy. However, if approved, treatment with this drug could also be more cost-effective due to decreased clinical support with fewer clinical visits. A study of Vivitrol among people addicted to heroin in Russia found a median 90% rate of opioid-free urines in the group receiving the medication versus 35% among controls; a 50% reduction in opioid craving versus no change for placebo; and a 75% longer retention in treatment for Vivitrol patients versus the control group. Such promising results could greatly impact the public health in Eastern Europe and Central Asia, where the intertwined epidemics of injection drug use and HIV [human immunodeficiency virus] are fueling devastating disease and societal disintegration, as well as here in the United States, particularly within the criminal justice system, where NIDA is currently studying Vivitrol's effectiveness.

Medication combinations have emerged as a promising strategy for treating addictions. This includes marijuana addiction, which accounts for approximately 4 million of the estimated 7 million Americans classified with dependence on or abuse of illicit drugs. Withdrawal symptoms—irritability, sleeplessness, increased appetite, drug craving—often prompt relapse in those trying to quit, but the combination of lofexi-dine (a medication to treat hypertension, approved in the U.K.) and dronabinol (an oral form of tetrahydrocannabinol (THC), the psychoactive ingredient in marijuana) has produced robust improvements in disordered sleep patterns, plus decreased marijuana withdrawal, craving, and relapse in daily marijuana smokers. Preliminary data also suggest the safety and possible efficacy of combined buprenorphine and naltrexone, for the treatment of cocaine addiction. Such findings are especially important since no medications currently exist for addiction to marijuana or addiction to cocaine.

Personalized approaches. Rapid advances in the science of genetics and related technologies are ushering in the age of personalized medicine, giving physicians and patients a greater understanding of health and disease at the molecular level. The field of pharmacogenetics, which deals with the influence of genetic variation on drug response in patients by correlating genetic polymorphisms and/or gene expression with drug efficacy, is opening up new worlds in addiction medicine possibilities. For example, a genetic variation has been identified that may help predict alcoholic patients' response to naltrexone (a μ-opioid receptor blocker). Specifically, a functional polymorphism of the μ-opioid receptor gene, found in about 15 to 25 percent of the general population, has been linked to naltrexone's efficacy in treating alcoholism; similar findings are also emerging in the treatment of nicotine addiction. As here, prescribing physicians may be able to improve and individualize patient treatment by taking genetic variation into account.

Current Obstacles to Innovative Solutions

New obstacles are appearing alongside existing ones, on both the medications development and service delivery fronts, that could restrain truly remarkable opportunities.

For instance, the cost of developing a new medication and bringing it to market can be, according to recent estimates, up to $2 billion. NIDA needs to leverage research and technical assistance in partnership with private entities to help bring a medication to market. Securing pharmaceutical industry involvement has been difficult, due largely to perceived financial disincentives. Many pharmaceutical companies have traditionally shied away from medications development for illicit drug disorders because of a relatively small patient population who also tend to be in lower income brackets, lack health insurance, or rely on the State for their care. Added to this is the stigma that still attaches to illicit drug addiction, along with concerns about this population's compromised health overall, which may present drug safety and other liability issues that further discourage pharmaceutical involvement. However, the implementation of the Mental Health Parity and Addiction Equity Act of 2008 and the increased accessibility to insurance coverage for those with lower incomes provided by the Affordable Care Act [of 2010] promise to expand access to substance abuse treatment and thereby open up the market for addiction medications. Moreover, capitalizing on new approaches that target brain circuits and molecules common to multiple addictions, including alcohol and tobacco, can also help increase market share, reduce stigma, and better engage pharmaceutical companies.

The reluctance of private companies to fully engage in the research and development of addiction medications has encumbered our ability to harness the full clinical potential of scientific discovery. But now, the problem is poised to worsen, as the pharmaceutical industry plans to reduce their investment in psychotherapeutics research and medications development. Not only does this situation impede the development of medications for mental illnesses generally, but it contracts the pool of available medications for secondary uses, including to treat drug addiction. This is a serious trend in a coun-

try where approximately one in four adults suffers from a di-
agnosable mental disorder in a given year and where, among
the 9.8 million adults with serious mental illness, 1 in 4 also
abuse or are dependent on illicit drugs or alcohol. This high
rate of comorbidity, together with fewer medications to treat
both illnesses, could adversely affect the public health.

Getting Treatments to People Who Need Them

While developing medications to treat addictions is important, access to these medications as well as other substance
abuse treatment services will be critical to improving outcomes for those struggling with substance abuse and addiction. It is a sad fact that more than 90% of the 23 million
Americans in need of treatment for substance use disorders
do not receive it. In addition, many treatments, including
nicotine replacement therapies, are not effective without behavioral therapies or social networks to help patients achieve
abstinence. NIDA is actively engaged in efforts to change this
situation, working through multiple venues, but especially the
medical community and the criminal justice system.

Engaging the Medical Community in Providing Treatment

Substance abuse is a chronic, relapsing medical disease. To
treat this disease effectively, we must—as a public health priority—promote the integration of addiction treatment into
the rest of the health care system. Failing to do so denies
addiction's probable complicity in and possible deleterious effects on other medical conditions or diagnoses. Mainstream-
ing substance abuse treatment requires that we engage primary care physicians, who are in a unique position to identify
drug use early and prevent its escalation to addiction and/or
to treat or refer patients with potential substance use prob-

Vaccinating Against Addictive Drug Use

Vaccines that would arm the immune system against addictive drugs and prevent them from making the user high are, potentially, the ultimate weapons against addiction. A cocaine vaccine is poised to enter its first large-scale clinical trial in humans this year [2008], and vaccines against nicotine, heroin and methamphetamine are also in development. In theory, these addiction vaccines work the same way as the traditional vaccines used to treat infectious diseases like measles and meningitis. But instead of targeting bacteria and viruses, the new vaccines zero in on addictive chemicals. Each of the proposed vaccines consists of drug molecules that have been attached to proteins from bacteria; it's the bacterial protein that sets off the immune reaction. Once a person has been vaccinated, the next time the drug is ingested, antibodies will latch onto it and prevent it from crossing from the bloodstream into the brain. . . . While the vaccine is being studied in people who are already addicted to cocaine, it could eventually be used on others. "You could vaccinate high-risk teens until they matured to an age of better decision-making," [Thomas] Kosten [of Baylor College of Medicine] says. He acknowledges the obvious civil-liberties issues this raises. "Lawyers certainly want to argue with us on the ethics of it," he says, "but parent groups and pediatricians have been receptive to the idea."

Janeen Interlandi, "What Addicts Need,"
Newsweek, *February 23, 2008.*

lems. Yet physicians tend not to prescribe proven addiction medications or to proactively identify potential problematic substance use in their patients. NIDA is working to change this circumstance through physician outreach and other initiatives.

Having addiction medications available could further engage the medical community in providing substance abuse treatment, helping patients recover from their substance use while also benefiting myriad other health conditions where drug use may affect the course and progression. We must therefore remain vigilant in our efforts to educate the health care community to properly screen for and treat substance use disorders.

Engaging the Criminal Justice System in Providing Treatment

Criminal justice settings offer prime venues for implementing evidence-based treatments among a high-risk population. More than half of incarcerated individuals have a substance use history, but rather than capitalizing on the opportunity to effectively treat this high-risk population, we continue to release prisoners without any provision or mechanism for follow-up treatment, in spite of known consequences: greater recidivism, relapse, and post-release mortality.

For example, more than 200,000 people addicted to heroin pass through American correctional facilities each year. Opioid maintenance therapy (e.g., methadone or buprenorphine) exemplifies a treatment that has proven effective in treating opioid dependence and in reducing drug-related disease and criminal recidivism. In a randomized clinical trial of methadone maintenance among 200 prisoners with pre-incarceration heroin dependence, those who received counseling plus methadone maintenance in prison with continued treatment in the community upon release were significantly less likely to be opioid- or cocaine-positive according to urine drug testing than those who received counseling only with passive referral or those who received counseling in prison with transfer to methadone upon release. Other research points to buprenor-phine treatment as a promising intervention for prisoners with heroin addiction histories and stresses that challenges related to dosing, administration, and regulation can be overcome via collaboration among treatment, research, and correctional personnel, particularly important at the Federal Government level (e.g., Federal Bureau of Prisons).

A lack of consistency in integrating effective treatments severely challenges our Nation's public health and safety agenda to reduce drug abuse and related crime. Therefore, we must provide community organizers, opinion leaders, and policy makers with the tools needed to, once and for all, neutralize the ideological practices that stigmatize substance use disorders, particularly as they affect criminal justice populations.

Cooperation Toward a Common Goal Is Vital

The combined neuroscientific discoveries of the last two decades [1990–2010] give us an unprecedented and detailed view of the risks, processes, and consequences of addiction. From this vantage point, scientists stand ready to test and develop a whole new generation of diverse pharmacotherapeutic agents to combat the devastating effects of drug addiction in more individualized and effective ways. As a result, we find ourselves at the threshold of incredible public health opportunities.

But scientific discovery is not enough. The scope and cost of the effort required to bring any successful new medications to market hinges on the unique synergism that can be generated when public-private partnerships focus on a common goal. In addition, to guarantee the success of such partnerships, we also need to work diligently to optimize the delivery of integrated health care that is responsive to new knowledge and to the particular features that characterize the disease of addiction.

> *"[Cognitive behavioral therapy] is an evidence-based form of psychotherapy that focuses on helping the patient to unlearn old drug-using or addictive behavior and learn to replace it with healthier behavior."*

Cognitive Behavior Therapy Helps in the Treatment of Addiction

Promises Treatment Centers

In the following viewpoint, Promises Treatment Centers, an addiction treatment center with locations in California and Texas, explains that the form of psychotherapy known as cognitive behavioral therapy (CBT) is a short-term approach to treatment that is based on the assumption that most behavioral and emotional reactions are learned and, therefore, can be unlearned. The goal of CBT is to enable patients to become aware of particular situations that often result in their addictive behavior, to avoid those situations if possible, and to learn healthier ways to react.

As you read, consider the following questions:

1. According to Promises Treatment Centers, how long does CBT treatment usually last?

2. Is CBT more ideal in group sessions or in one-on-one sessions between the therapist and client, according to Promises Treatment Centers?

3. Is CBT typically conducted on an outpatient basis or in a residential, inpatient setting, according to Promises Treatment Centers?

Overcoming addiction, getting unstuck from unhealthy behaviors, and moving on with your life is tough work. An individual dependent upon or addicted to substances can see a counselor for months or years to gain insights into why he or she abuses alcohol or drugs, engages in compulsive gambling, sex, or other addictive behaviors and still be stuck. After drying out or detoxification and undergoing treatment, however, without some solid strategies in their toolkit, the person will have a rough road ahead in recovery. While talking things out on an individual or group therapy basis is an integral part of the healing process, it's necessary to go beyond talk: Patients need to learn how to replace addictive behaviors.

Cognitive Behavioral Therapy

Cognitive behavioral therapy (CBT) is a form of psychotherapy that emphasizes the important role of thinking in how we feel and what we do, according to the National Association of Cognitive Behavioral Therapists (NACBT). The National Institute on Drug Abuse (NIDA) says CBT is a short term, focused approach to treatment that attempts to help patients recognize situations in which they are most likely to use drugs (or other substances or engage in other addictive behavior), avoid such situations when appropriate, and learn how to cope more effectively with a range of problems (and problematic behaviors) associated with substance abuse. . . .

- CBT . . . [takes] from 12 to 16 weeks. CBT is time-limited in that the patient is instructed at the outset of the therapy that there will be a point where the formal therapy process will end. This ending date of formal therapy is a mutually-arrived upon decision between the therapist and the patient. Therefore, CBT is not a never-ending treatment approach.

- Evidence of CBT's effectiveness in this short period of time makes it an attractive approach for clinicians to utilize—alone and in conjunction with other treatment modalities. CBT has been extensively evaluated in rigorous clinical trials and has solid empirical support as a treatment for cocaine abuse, for example. CBT has even proven effective for severely dependent cocaine abusers, according to NIDA data.

- CBT is structured and directive. Therapists have a specific agenda for each session and specific techniques or concepts are taught during each session. CBT is focused on the client's goals, not what the therapist thinks those goals should be. It is therefore directive in that CBT therapists show clients how to think and behave in ways to obtain their stated goals. The CBT therapist doesn't tell the patient what to do—they teach the patient how to do what it is they want to do (such as abstain from drug use).

- Flexibility is a key component of CBT. It can be readily adapted to a wide range of patients, settings that include inpatient or outpatient, and formats such as individual or group.

- CBT is a collaborative effort between the patient and the therapist. In order to be able to help the patient, the CBT therapist needs to learn what the patient wants out of life (his or her goals), and then help the patient achieve those goals. The CBT therapist listens, teaches, and encourages, while the role of the patient is expressing concerns, learning, and implementing.

- Speaking of the relationship between the CBT therapist and the client, a sound therapeutic relationship is necessary, but it isn't the focus of the treatment. A good, trusting relationship is the foundation, but there also has to be more. CBT therapists believe that their clients change because they learn how to think and act differently as a result of their learning. CBT, therefore, focuses on teaching rational self-counseling skills.

- CBT is compatible with a range of other forms of treatment the patient may receive, including pharmacotherapy, self-help groups such as Alcoholics Anonymous and Cocaine Anonymous, family and couples therapy, vocational counseling, parenting skills, and so on.

- CBT is based on an educational model. The therapy is based on the assumption that most behavioral and emotional reactions are learned. The goal of CBT, then, is to help patients unlearn maladaptive behavior and learn a new way of reacting that is healthier. The educational benefits of CBT lead to long-term results. When patients understand how and why they are doing well, they know what they need to do to continue those good outcomes.

- Homework is a central feature of CBT Patients need to complete reading assignments and practice what they've learned between sessions.

Key Components of CBT

There are two key components of CBT: functional analysis and skills training.

Functional Analysis: The patient and the CBT therapist work together to identify the feelings, thoughts, and circumstances of the patient before and after he or she drinks or uses drugs. This helps the patient to better understand the risks that will likely lead to a relapse. The functional analysis is critical, especially during the early treatment phase, for the patient and therapist to assess the high-risk situations that are likely to lead to drug use, as well as provide insights into why the patient may resort to using drugs. Some of the reasons may be coping with interpersonal difficulties, escaping from reality, or achieving euphoria not otherwise available in the patient's life. Further on in treatment, the functional analysis of episodes of drug or alcohol use may identify situations or states during which the patient continues to have difficulty coping.

Skills Training: Think of skills training as a way for patients to unlearn old habits and learn new and healthier behaviors to replace them. Treatment professionals say that by the time a person's drug habit is severe enough to warrant treatment, they have been using drugs as their primary means of coping with a wide range of interpersonal and intrapersonal problems. The reasons why include:

- They may never have learned effective strategies to deal with challenges in adult life. This is particularly true for those whose substance abuse began early in life (adolescence).

- Due to chronic involvement in a drug-using lifestyle, the individual may have forgotten effective strategies to deal with challenges and stresses. Constantly in drug-seeking, using, and recovering from the effects of drug use, the individual has repeatedly relied only on drug use as an effective coping mechanism.

- Although the individual may have learned effective strategies at one time, their ability to use them may be weakened by the presence of other problems, such as drug use and concurrent psychiatric disorder.

How CBT Works

When the patient (client) takes part in CBT, ideally, the session is just between the therapist and client. However, CBT can be modified to work in group sessions as well, as long as the session is structured to be long enough (at least 90 minutes, as compared to the normal 60 minute session length) so that each patient gets the opportunity to comment on their personal experience in trying out skills, give examples, and participate in role-playing.

The setting is typically an outpatient basis—although it is also effective in residential or inpatient settings. The outpatient setting, however, is preferred because it focuses on understanding what determines the patient's substance use, and this is best done in the context of the patient's day-to-day life. It's important for the CBT therapist to know where and how the individual lives, and who they are, so that individualized functional analyses can be created. The outpatient setting is also more conducive to the patient's practice of skills training learned during the sessions. They learn what does and doesn't work for them and discuss new strategies with their CBT therapist. . . .

Format of a Typical CBT Session

The flow of the CBT session (in a 60-minute session) may follow the 20-20-20 rule. Using this format, during the first 20 minutes the therapist focuses on the patient's substance abuse, cravings, and high-risk situations since the last session. The therapist listens and tries to elicit the patient's response, with the result that this portion of the session usually involves the patient doing most of the talking. In addition, the therapist seeks to find out how the practice of skills went in between the session (the patient's homework, based on what he/she

CBT as Part of an Overall Recovery Program

Cognitive-Behavioral Therapy (CBT) was developed as a method to prevent relapse when treating problem drinking, and later it was adapted for cocaine-addicted individuals. . . .

Research indicates that the skills individuals learn through cognitive-behavioral approaches remain after the completion of treatment. Current research focuses on how to produce even more powerful effects by combining CBT with medications for drug abuse and with other types of behavioral therapies. A computer-based CBT system has also been developed and has been shown to be effective in helping reduce drug use following standard drug abuse treatment.

National Institute on Drug Abuse,
Principles of Drug Addiction Treatment:
A Research-Based Guide, *3rd ed. Rockville, MD:*
National Institute on Drug Abuse, 2012.

learned in the previous session). The therapist may ask if the practice session was harder than expected, if the patient had any difficulties performing the practice, if he or she came up with any new strategies, and what worked well or did not work as well.

The second 20 minutes is devoted to the introduction and discussion of the topic for the particular session. In this segment, the therapist does most of the talking, although it is important that the therapist relate the material back to the patient and ensure he/she understands what's being introduced. A topic may be skills for refusing an offer of cocaine, or what to do in particularly high-risk situations. The therapist may ask if the patient understands the session material or how and why it relates to them, to describe the topic or skill in their own words, and role-play or practice the skill within the session.

Skill topics depend upon the substance abused (or addictive behavior) and are tailored to the patient's individual needs. As an example, there are eight skill topics for CBT for cocaine abuse. These include:

- Coping with craving

- Shoring up motivation and a commitment to stop

- Refusal skills/assertiveness

- Seemingly irrelevant decisions

- An all-purpose coping plan

- Problem solving

- Case management

- HIV risk reduction

The final 20 minutes involves the patient and therapist having a discussion about the topic introduced. Together, they agree on a practice exercise for the next week, and review plans for the next week and anticipate any high-risk situations.

Example of a Practice Exercise

Here is an example of a practice exercise for cocaine abuse. The patient is asked to write down or record his or her answers (as many answers as apply) to the following questions:

- Trigger—What sets me up to use cocaine?

- Thoughts and Feelings—What was I thinking? What was I feeling?

- Behavior—What did I do then?

- Positive Consequences—What positive thing happened?

- Negative Consequences—What negative thing happened?

Unlearn Old—Learn New

In summary, CBT is an evidence-based form of psychotherapy that focuses on helping the patient to unlearn old drug-using or addictive behavior and learn to replace it with healthier behavior. CBT works for some individuals, but not for others. CBT works best when used in combination with other recovery efforts. While it may be adapted for group use, it is considered most effective when used in a one-on-one therapist/patient basis. . . .

Remember that CBT is a structured and time-limited therapy, usually lasting 12 to 16 weeks. There may be booster sessions, as appropriate, and a long-term (one-year) follow-up that's part of the therapeutic process. As with other forms of therapy for drug abuse or addictive behavior, the motivation and determination of the patient to a life of abstinence in recovery is a crucial part of the process. By unlearning old behaviors and learning new ones, the road to recovery can be a lot easier to travel.

> *"Alcoholism and nutrition have a recip-*
> *rocal effect on one another that often*
> *pushes the alcoholic to relapse."*

Proper Nutrition Is Vital in Treating Alcoholism and Addiction

Cynthia Perkins

In the following viewpoint, Cynthia Perkins explains that after extended alcohol or drug use, the critical chemicals in the brain responsible for feelings of happiness and well-being are extensively damaged, and to achieve successful recovery, these chemicals must be brought into balance or cravings for alcohol or drugs will continue. Perkins maintains that good nutrition is essential in maintaining long-term sobriety. Cynthia Perkins is a holistic health counselor, sobriety coach, and author of the website Holistic Help.

As you read, consider the following questions:

1. According to Cynthia Perkins, what is one of the most common dietary deficiencies found in alcoholics?

2. Can a poor diet lead to drug addiction, according to Perkins?

3. According to Perkins, if people eat a proper diet but continue to consume alcohol, will their neurotransmitters remain balanced?

Understanding the relationship between nutrition and alcoholism is a vital component for successful recovery. Although many alcoholics become malnutritioned from their drinking and it's very important to eat a nutritious diet in recovery, this issue is much deeper than that.

Alcoholics are deficient in a variety of extremely important nutrients, which leads to imbalanced or depleted neurotransmitters in the brain and a sea of psychological and physiological symptoms that often result in relapse. Thus, identifying and correcting these deficiencies is another essential step in maintaining craving-free and long-term sobriety.

The role of nutrition and alcoholism is two pronged. On one hand, alcoholism causes nutritional deficiencies, while on the other hand nutritional deficiencies cause alcoholism. They have a reciprocal effect on one another that often pushes the alcoholic to relapse.

A poor diet that is high in sugar, refined foods and environmental toxins and lacking in vital nutrients, that the average person consumes these days, often results in nutritional deficiencies. Contrary to popular belief, vitamin and mineral deficiencies are quite common in our society and result in numerous uncomfortable and often debilitating symptoms.

On the most fundamental level, nutrients are needed to form neurotransmitters in the brain. Neurotransmitters are chemicals used by the brain to relay messages within the brain and communicate with all other organ systems within the body. An imbalance or deficiency in neurotransmitters, particularly dopamine, serotonin, GABA and endorphins have been found to be at the root of what causes addiction and cravings for alcohol and/or drugs.

The manufacturing process of neurotransmitters requires that very specific nutrients be present in precisely the right amount. If even one of these nutrients is absent for any reason, then neurons are not capable of producing adequate levels of neurotransmitters.

You'll want to read *understanding alcohol addiction* and *how to stop drinking alcohol* to understand this concept more completely. To achieve successful recovery from any addiction, neurotransmitters must be brought into balance, so understanding the interrelationship between nutrition and alcoholism is critical for achieving and maintaining lasting sobriety.

Symptoms and Impact of Deficiencies

Symptoms from a deficiency in vitamins, minerals, or amino acids may include depression, anxiety, hypoglycemia, fatigue, irritability, hyperactivity, insomnia, cognitive dysfunction, memory problems, learning disorders, personality disorders, hypertension, heart disease, headaches, agitation, cravings for sugar, caffeine, carbohydrates, nicotine, alcohol or drugs, and many more. You'll note that many of these symptoms look extremely similar to the symptoms that an alcoholic or addict in recovery experiences on a daily basis.

When your diet is deficient in the proper nutrients it needs, then your brain is deficient or out of balance in neurotransmitters. Those crucial chemicals are responsible for making you feel happy, relaxed and normal and they are not present or working efficiently. Your sense of well-being is in disaccord. You feel depressed, sad, anxious, tired, compulsive, confused, hyperactive and can't think clearly.

All psychotropic substances, including alcohol, mimic the effects of our neurotransmitters and thus provide us with a temporary, but artificial boost. When neurotransmitters are not balanced or deficient, then we crave things like alcohol, drugs, cigarettes, sugar and caffeine to give us relief and provide the feelings we should have naturally.

Since most people are eating a diet that is toxic and lacking in nutrients, nutritional deficiencies are usually present in the alcoholic or addict prior to addiction. It is one of the things that lead to addiction. We don't have enough dopamine, serotonin, GABA or endorphins, and drinking or drugs provides a temporary boost to those neurotransmitters, so it is actually giving us something we're missing. However, in the long run, the artificial stimulation of neurotransmitters only depletes them even further and leads to the much bigger problem of addiction.

To make matters worse, once alcoholism is set into motion, then the consumption of alcohol on a regular basis itself leads to more deficiencies from an even less nutritious diet and poor absorption. Alcoholics often drink in place of a meal or eat very little, and alcohol damages the body's ability to absorb the nutrients it needs from the food you do eat.

Alcoholism causes vitamin and mineral deficiencies because alcohol is toxic to the liver, pancreas, stomach and digestive tract, which results in damage that prevents the alcoholic from being able to digest their food properly or to store, absorb, process, access or absorb crucial nutrients. Many alcoholics are severely malnourished.

Additionally, financial limits may cause an alcoholic to have to choose between food or alcohol and alcohol usually always win the vote. As alcoholism progresses and the alcoholic loses their ability to make good choices, they could care less about the issue of nutrition and alcoholism. Unfortunately, the body will run on alcohol alone because it gives a temporary boost to the system; however, this only deprives the body of even more nutrients and sets up another vicious cycle.

Deficiencies create a variety of emotional and physical symptoms that make the alcoholic crave a drink in order to relieve the symptoms. Not only that, deficiencies themselves contribute to deterioration in the integrity of the digestive tract which results in more inability to absorb nutrients. The drink perpetuates the problem of deficiencies in a variety of ways.

Common Nutritional Deficiencies Found in the Drug and Alcohol Addicted

Regardless of which came first, addiction or nutritional deficiencies, some of the most common deficiencies found in alcoholics include: amino acids, essential fatty acids, digestive enzymes, acetyl coenzyme A, niacin or B3, B6, B2, B12, folic acid, NAD, vitamins A, C, D, and K, magnesium, zinc, selenium and calcium, and have a profound impact on brain chemistry and mood. The lack of awareness around nutrition and alcoholism often results with alcoholics in recovery who struggle to stay sober because of the need to find relief from the discomfort that deficiencies cause.

One of the most common deficiencies found in alcoholics, and addicts of all kinds, and the most crucial to address is amino acids. Amino acids are the building blocks for neurotransmitters. You can't have balanced neurotransmitters if you aren't consuming adequate amino acids. Additionally, amino acids work in conjunction with numerous other vitamin and minerals to perform their functions adequately.

For example, sertonin production requires tryptophan, iron, niacin, folic acid and B6; while dopamine requires tyrosine, iron, niacin, folic acid and B6; and GABA synthesis needs glutamine and B6, and endorphins.

Essential fatty acids are needed in the replenishment of all neurotransmitters, as they are essential for proper neurotransmission, meaning the movement of neurotransmitters from neuron to neuron; they affect the speed and strength of transmission. Fatty acids are also critical in the formation of new brain cells (neurons) and to repair damaged ones, so they are crucial to repair neurons that may have been damaged from your substance of choice.

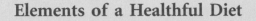

Elements of a Healthful Diet

A healthful, balanced diet provides your body with the nutritional tools it needs to heal quickly and effectively. Eating regularly, drinking sufficient amounts of fluids, and consuming a highly nutritious diet can help to:

- furnish sufficient energy for recovery

- decrease alcohol and drug cravings

- improve sleep quality and duration

- increase mental concentration

- decrease withdrawal-related anxiety and depression

- stabilize weight

- normalize hunger and satiety signals

Harold C. Urschel,
Healing the Addicted Brain.
Naperville, IL: Sourcebooks, 2009.

Vitamin B1 or thiamin is crucial for proper functioning of the brain and nerves, essential for the production of adenosine triphosphate (ATP) bioenergy in all body cells and the production of acetylcholine, the brains major neurotransmitter. A lack of adequate acetylcholine is found in disorders such as Alzheimer's. A deficiency in vitamin B1 leads to the syndrome often found in chronic alcoholics called Wernicke-Korsakoff syndrome and is distinguished by poor memory, impaired neuromuscular coordination, visual disturbances, apathy and mental confusion. Even a mild deficiency in this vitamin can result in impaired brain function and be exhibited in symptoms such as fatigue, emotional instability, confusion, indifference or lack of interest, headaches, depression, irritability, feelings of impending doom and insomnia.

NAD (the active form of B3) is critical for burning sugar and fat into energy for the cells, and it functions as a catalyst in the production of many of the major brain neurotransmitters like serotonin.

The most severe form of niacin (also known as B3) deficiency results in the disease known as pellagra, however, even a mild deficiency will produce a host of psychological symptoms including an inability to concentrate, excessive worry, headaches, irrational or unfounded fear and suspicion, apprehension, gloomy angry or depressed perception, agitation and disruption of sleep patterns.

Acetyl coenzyme A is probably the most crucial biochemical involved in cellular biochemistry, because it's needed to power the Krebs cycle, which is what produces 90 percent of all energy needed for every cell in the brain and the body. It's also needed to produce acetylcholine, the brain's major neurotransmitter that is critical for memory, learning and concentration.

A deficiency in B6 is significant because it is the primary coenzyme essential to produce all the chief brain neurotransmitters. It's crucial to many different conversion processes in amino acids, essential fatty acids and other important vitamins like B3 or niacin and helps regulate the entry of magnesium into our cells.

On the other hand, too much of a particular nutrient can also result in disrupted brain function and cravings for the substance of choice as well. For example, too much copper impairs neurotransmitter production and depletes zinc levels; however, copper is also needed in the production of many neurotransmitters. Balance is the key. Excess copper is commonly found in the addicted population.

Correcting Nutritional Deficiencies

It is possible for deficiencies and neurotransmitters to normalize on their own in a few years, if one is eating the right diet, but cravings will interfere in the process before the goal is achieved. So a variety of nutritional supplements are used to provide the brain with a temporary boost in nutrients so that the brain can replenish depleted neurotransmitters more quickly.

Nutritional supplements provide the brain with the raw materials it needs to replenish neurotransmitters more rapidly than diet alone, which ultimately aids in the detoxification process, reduces withdrawal, eliminates cravings and prevents relapse.

Research using brain imagery scans has shown that neurotransmitter activity is increased with IV nutritional supplementation and consequently withdrawal is alleviated. Treatment centers that repair brain chemistry using nutritional therapies have a success rate of 74 percent to 90 percent. Thus, your chances of remaining clean and sober are significantly higher when you use nutritional therapy.

However, the primary place you should get your nutrients is your diet. Supplements should be used temporarily to support the diet. If you do not make the necessary changes in diet to support healthy neurotransmitter production and function, then you are not likely to see long-term success with nutritional supplements.

In *End Your Addiction Now*, Dr. Charles Gant, an addiction expert, tells us, "Poor nutrition is one of the critical risk factors for substance abuse, and if you ignore your diet, you're putting yourself at risk for relapse, even if you continue to take nutritional supplements." Furthermore from Dr. Gant, "a diet high in carbohydrates increases the likelihood of substance abuse," and if you eat a lot of carbohydrates or junk food you may find it difficult to remain substance free even if you continue nutritional supplements.

I could not agree more. In my own personal experience, I have found there is nothing more significant in the recovery from addiction than the diet. As a matter of fact, it is the foundation on which everything else is built and can make or break your success. It is where most of your focus should be aimed.

Changes in my diet and lifestyle completely eliminated cravings for alcohol, nicotine, caffeine, marijuana, benzodiazepines, sugar and carbs. At the time this page was written, it has enabled me to achieve 25 years of uninterrupted and craving-free sobriety.

One of the primary reasons that addicts fail to maintain sobriety for their drug of choice is because of their diet.

The brain needs a consistent supply of nutrients on a day-to-day basis from the diet to continue to make neurotransmitters and perform optimal transmission. If nutrient levels are not maintained and/or the wrong types of food are consumed, then neurotransmitter levels will decline and disruption of mood, thought and behavior and the inevitable cravings for alcohol or the substance of choice will return.

The wrong types of foods actually deplete and/or disrupt the neurotransmitters even further. Sugar, caffeine, refined junk food, food additives and preservatives, artificial flavorings, sweeteners and coloring, white flour, and even complex carbohydrates like whole grains and potatoes, all impact the brain in a similar manner as alcohol and hard drugs and they need to be avoided. They produce an intense surge in neurotransmitters and insulin and the inevitable crash and depletion. They simulate and perpetuate the addiction cycle.

You can find a more in-depth discussion about the diet that is needed for overcoming alcoholism or any other addiction in my *Diet for Sobriety guidelines*, that is part of my Clean and Sober for Life Jump-Start Program, but basically we need to eat foods that will provide the proper amino acids, vitamins, minerals and fatty acids so the brain can begin to make its neurotransmitters on its own again and they can function adequately, and avoid foods that disrupt and deplete neurotransmitters. The diet that fulfills these criteria is a slightly modified version of the Paleolithic diet and consists of meat, fish, eggs, low-starch vegetables, and a small amounts of nuts, seeds and low-sugar fruit; butter and yogurt may be used if there is not a dairy intolerance.

All this biochemistry talk about nutrition and alcoholism can get a little technical and difficult to understand, but the bottom line is this: Nutritional deficiencies, regardless of when they originated, result in a malfunctioning brain and body that gets exhibited in a variety of undesirable and even dangerous psychological and physical symptoms. When we look over the list of symptoms that are the result of nutritional deficiencies, we see the typical profile of an alcoholic and addicts of all kinds. When the recovering alcoholic or addict understands the importance of addiction, alcoholism and nutrition and addresses their nutritional deficiencies, they can alleviate the cravings to drink or drunk and the psychological symptoms that so often lead to relapse.

Periodical and Internet Sources Bibliography

The following articles have been selected to supplement the diverse views presented in this chapter.

Steve Balt	"Why Psychiatrists Don't Treat Addicts," The Carlat Psychiatry Blog, November 20, 2011.
Richard Levak	"Individuals Have Ability to Conquer Addictions," *U-T San Diego*, February 22, 2013.
Mayo Clinic Staff	"Intervention: Help a Loved One Overcome Addiction," Mayo Clinic, August 23, 2011.
Jeanne McAlister	"Changing the Conversation About Addiction," *U-T San Diego*, January 1, 2013.
Jesse McKinley	"Doctors Seek New Approach for Jailed Addicts," *New York Times*, May 20, 2012.
John R. Murphy	"De-Felonization: My Approach to Reducing the Cost of Incarcerating Addicts," *Barrister*, 2013.
Catherine New	"The Real Tab for Rehab: Inside the Addiction Treatment Biz," *Daily Finance*, June 3, 2011.
Charles P. O'Brien	"If Addictions Can Be Treated, Why Aren't They?" Dana Foundation, June 2012.
Douglas Quenqua	"An Addiction Vaccine, Tantalizingly Close," *New York Times*, October 3, 2011.
Douglas Quenqua	"Rethinking Addiction's Roots and Its Treatment," *New York Times*, July 10, 2011.
Shari Roan	"Treatment for Addicts Is Starting to Change," *Los Angeles Times*, September 22, 2012.
Lloyd I. Sederer	"Addiction: Help You Can Get Beyond 12-Step and Conventional Western Medications," *The Huffington Post*, July 16, 2012.

For Further Discussion

Chapter 1

1. Many Americans believe that marijuana should be legalized for medical use. After reading the viewpoints of the California Society of Addiction Medicine and Paul Armentano, do you agree or disagree? Are there any safety risks to the public that concern you? Defend your answer.

2. Kimberly Young writes about the addictive risks involved with online role-playing games; however, Peter Gray insists the risks have been considerably overblown. Whose evidence do you find more compelling? Explain your answer.

Chapter 2

1. Some of the viewpoints in this chapter discuss drug-screening programs, such as student questionnaires and drug testing, to prevent addiction. Based on what you have read, do you think screening programs are effective? Why or why not?

2. John M. McCardell Jr. believes young people should learn responsible drinking habits before they reach the age of twenty-one. Toben F. Nelson and his coauthors, however, maintain that lowering the legal drinking age will increase alcohol-related problems. Which argument do you believe is more convincing and why?

3. Many people believe that putting restrictions on the marketing and sale of tobacco products and that increasing the tobacco tax will prevent young people from starting to smoke and will encourage active smokers to quit. In your opinion, do you think tobacco restrictions will have any effect on youth smoking? What do you think about a tobacco tax increase? Explain your answer.

Chapter 3

1. Patrick A. Trueman believes the addictive effects of pornography damages lives and relationships, while Milton Diamond insists pornography is not harmful and, in fact, can actually be beneficial. Which argument do you believe is more convincing? Explain your answer.

2. After reading the viewpoint of Lance Dodes, do you agree that addicted parents have a detrimental impact on their children? Are there any safety risks to these children that concern you? Explain your answer.

Chapter 4

1. Some of the authors in this chapter discuss twelve-step recovery programs. In your opinion, are twelve-step programs beneficial or detrimental in healing addiction? Explain your answer.

Organizations to Contact

The editors have compiled the following list of organizations concerned with the issues debated in this book. The descriptions are derived from materials provided by the organizations. All have publications or information available for interested readers. The list was compiled on the date of publication of the present volume; names, addresses, phone and fax numbers, and email and Internet addresses may change. Be aware that many organizations take several weeks or longer to respond to inquiries, so allow as much time as possible.

Adult Children of Alcoholics World Service Organization (ACA WSO)
PO Box 3216, Torrance, CA   90510
(562) 595-7831
website: http://adultchildren.org

Adult Children of Alcoholics World Service Organization (ACA WSO) is a nonprofit organization devoted to supporting adult children of alcoholics and otherwise dysfunctional families. Using the twelve-step program developed by Alcoholics Anonymous, ACA WSO helps its members better understand how their childhood experiences affect their adult relationships. The ACA WSO website offers information on meetings and events, newsletters, and articles.

Al-Anon Family Groups
1600 Corporate Landing Parkway, Virginia Beach, VA   23454
(757) 563-1600 • fax: (757) 563-1655
e-mail: wso@al-anon.org
website: www.al-anon.alateen.org

Al-Anon Family Groups is a fellowship of men, women, and children whose lives have been affected by an alcoholic family member or friend. Members share their experiences, strength, and hope to help each other and to help in the recovery of the alcoholic. Al-Anon's publications include *Al-Anon Faces Alcoholism* and *A Guide for Families of Al-Anon Members*, as well as the monthly magazine *Forum*.

Alcoholics Anonymous (A.A.)

PO Box 459, New York, NY   10163
(212) 870-3400
website: www.aa.org

Alcoholics Anonymous (A.A.) is an international fellowship of people who are recovering from alcoholism. Because A.A.'s primary goal is to help alcoholics remain sober, it does not sponsor research or engage in education about alcoholism. A.A. does publish a catalog of literature concerning the organization, including the books *Alcoholics Anonymous: The Big Book* and *Twelve Steps and Twelve Traditions*, as well as several pamphlets, such as *Is A.A. for You?* and *This is A.A.—An Introduction to the A.A. Recovery Program*.

American Society of Addiction Medicine (ASAM)

4601 North Park Avenue, Upper Arcade #101
Chevy Chase, MD   20815
(301) 656-3920 • fax: (301) 656-3815
e-mail: email@asam.org
website: www.asam.org

The American Society of Addiction Medicine (ASAM) is an organization of researchers, physicians, and other professionals who seek to educate health-care providers and the public about ways of treating and preventing addiction. It carries out its mission by sponsoring research and publishing annual reports. ASAM also publishes *ASAM Magazine*, the quarterly *Journal of Addiction Medicine*, and the weekly *ASAM Weekly*.

Law Enforcement Against Prohibition (LEAP)

121 Mystic Avenue, Medford, MA   02155
(781) 393-6985 • fax: (781) 393-2964
e-mail: info@leap.cc
website: www.leap.cc

Founded on March 16, 2002, Law Enforcement Against Prohibition (LEAP) is a nonprofit organization made up of current and former members of the law enforcement and criminal justice communities. The mission of LEAP is to educate the public, the media, and policy makers about the failure of current drug policy and to reform drug laws so that the sale and distribution of drugs would be regulated by a government body. LEAP publishes videos, press releases, and documents, including "End Prohibition Now!" and "Why I Want All Drugs Legalised."

National Association for Children of Alcoholics (NACoA)
10920 Connecticut Avenue, Suite 100, Kensington, MD 20895
(888) 554-2627 • fax: (301) 468-0987
e-mail: nacoa@nacoa.org
website: www.nacoa.org

The National Association for Children of Alcoholics (NACoA) is a nonprofit organization that advocates for children of parents who are dependent on alcohol and drugs. It accomplishes its mission by raising public awareness of the effects of parental drug dependence on children and by influencing legislation on local and federal levels. NACoA regularly publishes informative articles and booklets, such as *The Hidden Pain of the Addicted Family*; and *Children of Addiction*.

National Center for Responsible Gaming (NCRG)
1299 Pennsylvania Avenue, NW, Suite 1175
Washington, DC 20004
(202) 552-2689 • fax: (202) 552-2676
e-mail: info@ncrg.org
website: www.ncrg.org

The National Center for Responsible Gaming (NCRG) is the only national organization exclusively devoted to funding research that helps increase understanding of pathological and youth gambling and find effective methods of treatment for the disorder. NCRG produces the monthly online column "Issues & Insights" and provides links to programs aimed at young people, including Talking with Children About Gambling and Facing the Odds: The Mathematics of Gambling and Other Risks.

National Center on Addiction and Substance Abuse at Columbia University (CASAColumbia)

633 Third Avenue, Nineteenth Floor, New York, NY   10017
(212) 841-5200
website: www.casacolumbia.org

The National Center on Addiction and Substance Abuse at Columbia University (CASAColumbia) informs Americans of the economic and social costs of substance use and addiction and its impact on their lives; assesses what works in prevention, treatment and disease management; and encourages every individual and institution to take responsibility to reduce these health problems. CASAColumbia strives to provide health-care providers, policy makers and individuals with the tools they need to succeed and to remove the stigma of addiction. The organization publishes books, occasional papers, a newsletter, and reports, such as *National Survey of American Attitudes on Substance Abuse XVII: Teens* and *Addiction Medicine: Closing the Gap Between Science and Practice.*

National Council on Alcoholism and Drug Dependence (NCADD)

217 Broadway, Suite 712, New York, NY   10017
(212) 269-7797 • fax: (212) 269-7510
e-mail: national@ncadd.org
website: www.ncadd.org

Founded in 1944, the National Council on Alcoholism and Drug Dependence (NCADD) provides education, information, and assistance to the public and health-care providers about alcohol and drug addiction. It advocates prevention, intervention, and treatment through a nationwide network of affiliates. In addition to videos, posters, and fact sheets, NCADD publishes brochures, such as *Drinking Too Much Too Fast Can Kill You* and *Girls! Straight Talk About Drinking and Drugs.*

National Council on Problem Gambling (NCPG)

730 Eleventh Street, NW, Suite 601, Washington, DC   20001
(202) 547-9204 • fax: (202) 547-9206
e-mail: ncpg@ncpgambling.org
website: www.ncpgambling.org

The mission of the National Council on Problem Gambling (NCPG) is to increase public awareness of pathological gambling, to ensure the widespread availability of treatment for problem gamblers and their families, and to encourage research and programs for prevention and education. The NCPG and its thirty-three state affiliates have a variety of gambling-related resources available through its website, including a search feature for locating nationally certified counselors, a list of scheduled continuing education unit courses and resources, press releases, and a discussion forum. The NCPG also operates a confidential twenty-four-hour, toll-free helpline: (800) 522-4700.

National Institute on Drug Abuse (NIDA)

6001 Executive Boulevard, Room 5213, MSC 9561
Bethesda, MD   20892
(301) 443-1124
website: www.drugabuse.gov

The National Institute on Drug Abuse (NIDA) is one of the National Institutes of Health, part of the U.S. Department of Health and Human Services. Its mission is to use science to help understand and treat drug addiction. It accomplishes this goal by sponsoring and disseminating research and by working with legislators and other lawmakers through its advisory group, the National Advisory Council on Drug Abuse. In addition to fact sheets and brief research reports, NIDA publishes the newsletter *What's New at NIDA* as well as full-text publications on a range of topics, including *Drugs, Brains, and Behavior: The Science of Addiction*.

Nicotine Anonymous (NicA)

6333 East Mockingbird #147-817, Dallas, TX   75214

e-mail: info@nicotine-anonymous.org
website: www.nicotine-anonymous.org

Nicotine Anonymous (NicA) is a nonprofit national support organization that uses the twelve-step program developed by Alcoholics Anonymous to help members quit smoking. In addition to regular meetings across the country, NicA offers outreach services to community members addicted to nicotine. Its publications include pamphlets, such as *A Nicotine User's View of the Twelve Steps* and *Tips for Gaining Freedom from Nicotine.*

Overeaters Anonymous (OA)

PO Box 44020, Rio Rancho, NM 87174
(505) 891-2664 • fax: (505) 891-4320
website: www.oa.org

Founded in 1960, Overeaters Anonymous (OA) is a national support group that uses the twelve-step program developed by Alcoholics Anonymous to help members better understand their struggles with a variety of disordered eating behaviors. In addition to regular group meetings across the country, OA provides outreach services and education to the public. OA publishes the quarterly newsletter *A Step Ahead*, the monthly newsletter *The Courier* for professionals, and *Lifeline Magazine.*

Secular Organizations for Sobriety (SOS)

4773 Hollywood Boulevard, Hollywood, CA 90027
(323) 666-4295
e-mail: sos@cfiwest.org
website: www.cfiwest.org/SOS

Secular Organizations for Sobriety (SOS), also known as Save Our Selves, is a nonprofit network of autonomous, nonprofessional local groups in the United States and many European countries dedicated to helping individuals achieve and maintain sobriety. SOS began as a secular alternative to sobriety programs focused on God or some other higher power. The

SOS website provides a number of resources, including online support groups, a sobriety tool kit, news and updates, and the quarterly *SOS International Newsletter*.

Bibliography of Books

Allen Berger

12 Stupid Things That Mess Up Recovery: Avoiding Relapse Through Self-Awareness and Right Action. Center City, MN: Hazelden, 2008.

Michael Bradley

When Things Get Crazy with Your Teen: The Why, the How, and What to Do Now. New York: McGraw-Hill, 2009.

Jennifer Bruha

The Adolescent Relapse Prevention Planner. San Francisco: Turning Stone, 2012.

Gary Paul Byrne

The Drug Attraction: What Parents Need to Know to Keep Kids Out of Trouble. East Grinstead, UK: Drive4Life, 2011.

Greg Campbell

Pot, Inc.: Inside Medical Marijuana, America's Most Outlaw Industry. New York: Sterling, 2012.

Patrick J. Carnes

A Gentle Path Through the Twelve Steps: The Classic Guide for All People in the Process of Recovery. Center City, MN: Hazelden, 2012.

Nicholas Carr

The Shallows: What the Internet Is Doing to Our Brains. New York: Norton, 2010.

George N. Collins

Breaking the Cycle: Free Yourself from Sex Addiction, Porn Obsession, and Shame. Oakland, CA: New Harbinger, 2010.

Beverly Conyers   *Everything Changes: Help for Families of Newly Recovering Addicts.* Center City, MN: Hazelden, 2009.

Tian Dayton   *The ACOA Trauma Syndrome: The Impact of Childhood Pain on Adult Relationships.* Deerfield Beach, FL: Health Communications, 2012.

Andrew P. Doan   *Hooked on Games: The Lure and Cost of Video Game and Internet Addiction.* Coralville, IA: FEP International, 2012.

Steve Fox, Paul Armentano, and Mason Tvert   *Marijuana Is Safer: So Why Are We Driving People to Drink?* White River Junction, VT: Chelsea Green, 2009.

James P. Gray   *Why Our Drug Laws Have Failed and What We Can Do About It*, 2nd ed. Philadelphia: Temple University Press, 2012.

Gene M. Heyman   *Addiction: A Disorder of Choice.* Boston: Harvard University Press, 2009.

Peggy Kern   *Bluford High #14: No Way Out.* New York: Townsend, 2009.

Morteza Khaleghi and Karen Khaleghi   *The Anatomy of Addiction: Overcoming the Triggers That Stand in the Way of Recovery.* New York: Palgrave Macmillan, 2011.

Martin A. Lee   *Smoke Signals: A Social History of Marijuana—Medical, Recreational, and Scientific.* New York: Scribner, 2012.

Jamie Marich	*Trauma and the Twelve Steps: A Complete Guide for Enhancing Recovery*. North Charleston, SC: Cornersburg Media, 2012.
Jane Middleton-Moz and Lorie Dwinell	*After the Tears: Helping Adult Children of Alcoholics Heal Their Childhood Trauma*. Deerfield Beach, FL: Health Communications, 2010.
Cindy L. Miller-Perrin, Ola W. Barnett, and Robin D. Perrin	*Family Violence Across the Lifespan: An Introduction*. Thousand Oaks, CA: Sage, 2011.
Bill Oliver	*Raising Teens in a Toxic World*. Merritt Island, FL: Passage Group, 2008.
Lawrence Peltz	*The Mindful Path to Addiction Recovery: A Practical Guide to Regaining Control over Your Life*. Boston: Shambhala Publications, 2013.
Trish Regan	*Joint Ventures: Inside America's Almost Legal Marijuana Industry*. Hoboken, NJ: Wiley, 2011.
Kevin Roberts	*Cyber Junkie: Escape the Gaming and Internet Trap*. Center City, MN: Hazelden, 2010.
Natasha Dow Schull	*Addiction by Design: Machine Gambling in Las Vegas*. Princeton, NJ: Princeton University Press, 2012.
Howard Shaffer	*Change Your Gambling, Change Your Life*. San Francisco: Jossey-Bass, 2012.

Sam Skolnik   *High Stakes: The Rising Cost of*
                   America's Gambling Addiction.
                   Boston: Beacon, 2011.

Harold C. Urschel *Healing the Addicted Brain.*
                   Naperville, IL: Sourcebooks, 2009.

Martina Watts   *Nutrition and Addiction.* Brighton,
                   England: Pavilion, 2011.

Index